Get Knitting!

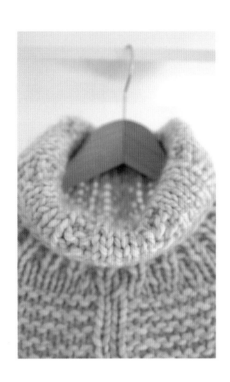

Created by **Lynn Bryan, The BookMaker, London**
Design by **Rachel Gibson**
Location photography by **Amanda Hancocks**
Studio photography by **James Duncan**
Illustrations by **Conny Jude**

STERLING and the distinctive Sterling logo are
registered trademarks of Sterling Publishing Co., Inc.

**Library of Congress Cataloging-in-Publication
Data Available**

10   9   8   7   6   5   4   2

Previously published as *Start to Knit*.
Published by Sterling Publishing Co., Inc.
387 Park Avenue South
New York, NY 10016 USA
© 2005 Gina Macris
Distributed in Canada by
Sterling Publishing Company
c/o Canadian Manda Group, 165 Dufferin Street
Toronto, Ontario, Canada M6K 3H6
Distributed in the United Kingdom by
GMC Distribution Services
Castle Place, 166 High Street, Lewes, East Sussex,
England BN7 1XU
Distributed in Australia by
Capricorn Link (Australia) Pty. Ltd.
P.O. Box 704, Windsor, NSW 2756, Australia

Sterling ISBN 978-1-4027-1650-8 (hardcover)

Sterling ISBN 978-1-4027-5392-3 (paperback)

For information about custom editions, special sales,
premium and corporate purchases, please contact
Sterling Special Sales Department at 800-805-5489
or specialsales@sterlingpublishing.com.

Get Knitting!

Gina Macris

STERLING

New York / London

www.sterlingpublishing.com

Introduction   6

**Yarns and Basic
Tools   12**

Get Knitting   22
Casting On, Knit Stitch,
Purl Stitch, Holding the
Yarn, Knit & Purl Stitch
Library, Binding Off,
Shaping with Increases and
Decreases, Stitch Gauge,
Reading the Pattern, Fit

The Finishing Touch   42
Blocking, Seaming, Picking Up
Stitches, Correcting Errors,
Borders & Embellishments,
Buttonholes, Glossary,
Abbreviations, Caring for Your
Garments,

THE PROJECTS   60

A Long, Fringed
Scarf 62

A Short Silken Scarf
64

A Hat with a Rolled
Brim 66

A Boatneck Sweater
68

Shaping Up: More Skills

A Sleeveless Summer
Top 72

A Perfect Poncho 76

An Elegant Casual
Cardigan 80

A Sophisticated
Evening Bag 84

CONTENTS

An Openwork Scarf
88

A Cute Topper   90

A Circular Hat with
Earflaps 94

Basic Cabling 98
An Easy Way to Cable
A Man's Sweater 102

Knitting for Young Ones 108

A Kimono Wrap 110

Baby Booties 114

Mosaic Knitting   118   Index 126
A Girl's Cardigan 120   Acknowledgments 128

INTRODUCTION

Knitting has been a constant companion of mine ever since I was eight years old. My yarns have become a thread through my life. For me, nothing can be more satisfying than seeing one ball of yarn after another become a beautiful fabric in my hands, stitch by stitch.

I have taken my knitting everywhere; on the train, the plane, the boat and the car—even to a baseball game. Three decades ago, I saw the English countryside from the passenger's seat of a Morris Mini, with real Shetland wool in my hands. When I stood in an endless line outside the Statue of Liberty in New York with my young son and his friend nearly a decade ago, the beginnings of a multi-colored waistcoat accompanied me. My little boy and his pal, who ducks in doorways these days, are now ready to enter college. And I knit on.

I don't mean to imply that I began as an adventurous knitter or even a good one. On the contrary. The early stitches were all uneven, and I quickly learned which combinations of knit and purl softened the imperfections and which ones made me want to gnash my teeth and r-r-rip it all out!

Then there was the mystery of size. I couldn't be bothered to stop and figure out this thing called "gauge," the knitted sample–before-the-sweater that predicted the finished size. Whether my sweaters fit or not was strictly a matter of wishful thinking.

Now I tell people that the reason they like my knitting is that I've already made all the really bad mistakes and learned from them. One of the things I love about knitting is that the mistakes are reversible. And knitting reminds me that so much about learning is practice. This is the only way I became a knitter of even stitches. Practice. In my mid-twenties I decided I was going to even out the stitches and make things fit or hang it up.

I bought the rust-colored Shetland wool and began a cardigan, forcing myself to wrap the yarn around the fingers of my right hand in consistent

fashion. It was excruciating to unlearn the haphazard way I had of "throwing" yarn and to learn all over again, my fingers suddenly awkward and fumbling. But the new way of knitting got a tiny bit easier each day, and I was pleased enough with the results to make a deal with myself that I would learn one new thing on each project from that moment on.

Eventually, my knitting became as complicated as my life, crowded with the demands of marriage, a career, a home, and finally, children. Even in the most hectic days, as my two boys were growing up, I always managed to make time for knitting, if only twenty minutes in the early morning, when the house was dark and quiet and I had my first cup of coffee.

There did come a time when I had to rein in the amount of yarn that was accumulating, especially after a huge sale that netted me enough designer wool for several sweaters. Most of it is still in boxes. Bent over intricate colorwork done in very small stitches, I refused to face how much time I did not have to knit. Instead, I kept myself out of yarn shops, and missed the early harbingers of change. The new knitting didn't creep up on me so much as walk up and smack me in the face.

When I finally woke up, I saw fibers that dazzled the eye, beckoned the hand, and banished restraint. Today, the colors alone can bring on a knitter's high. There are hand-dyed yarns that stripe themselves in colorways so breathtaking that it seems only someone who has attained complete harmony and balance could have created them. The yarns bring home the hues of cool mountain vistas, sunbaked adobe villages, brilliant sunsets, and more.

And each new yarn is softer and silkier than the last, with natural and synthetic fibers combined in seductive textural effects. Looking at yarns also means touching them. Eyes, hands, and spirit feast on them. One day it took me an entire delicious hour of savoring the possibilities to pick out two strands for a simple scarf, one a mohair of subtle purples and blues, and the other a thin filament sporting little square flags. The little flags both gave a nod to the shades of mohair and added their own glimmering contrast.

I love seeing women with silver hair fingering yarn that looks like a bundle of froth. The gesture says, "See, I'm not too old to have this kind of fun!" Young or old, it's common to see people coming out to look at yarn in pairs. One is the knitter and the other is the mother, daughter, husband, or friend who will wear

the finished piece. These pairs remind me that knitting is about love and friendship. The knitting will forever become entwined with the relationship between the one who gives and the one who receives.

The number of beginners has been expanding in the last several years for many reasons, starting with the mesmerizing fibers. I like to think of myself as a new knitter as well. After all those tiny stitches, I'm magnetized by the quick gratification of a wrap or hat knit in a splash of fuzzy color on big needles. And I'm learning that there's always more to learn, as I look at knit and purl and all the rest in entirely new ways. For me, it expands the fun and makes me feel as if I were discovering something for the very first time.

I hope to share some of that enthusiasm with you in the following pages, beginning with an understanding of different yarns and needles and other helpful tools. Some basic skills will allow you to knit simple items that only look complicated, thanks to yarns that do all the work. A glossary of terms and abbreviations you'll see written in patterns, a guide to the types of stitches you may want to use are also included in the basics chapter. My job is to help you de-mystify the process of knitting by breaking it down into clear, manageable

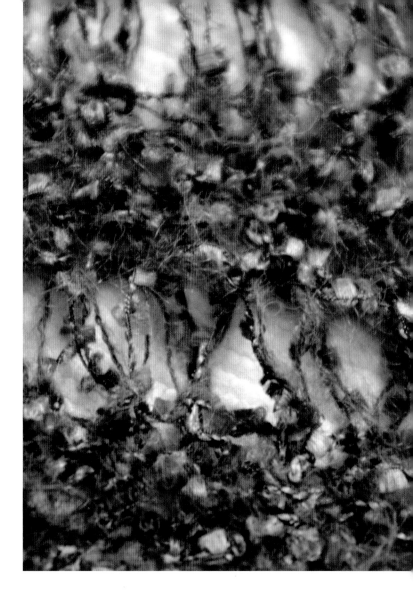

steps. When you're ready, you'll see how learning to shape your knitting, by increasing and decreasing stitches, will enable you to greatly expand your choices. A diagram of the body and how to make garments fit is also featured. And because everyone learns at a different pace, I've included both easy-to-knit and fashionable projects for the beginner and some for the more adventurous knitters among you. Whether you're knitting for the very first time or have learned to make classic cables, the idea is to have fun.

I've learned a lot and met some wonderful people as I've worked on this book. One thing I especially like about knitting today is the way it brings people together, either online or in person. Ad-hoc knitting groups are everywhere, inviting people to make time for conversation and clicking needles, or clicking needles alone, if that's what suits the group. For me, knitting is both shared experience and solitary practice, a journey where the hands acquire their own memory. Most of all, knitting is the stillness of the moment, keeping time and care at bay.

GINA MACRIS

YARNS AND BASIC TOOLS

The yarn you select shapes your knitting in many ways.

Understanding fiber lets you select a yarn that is fun to knit

and fits the style of your project. The right needles and a

well-organized collection of tools also help make

a pleasure out of knitting. This chapter

explores your options.

———————

YARNS

*Much of the yarn available comes from renewable natural resources;
animals that grow a new coat every year as well as plants like cotton and
flax. Synthetics have also moved to the cutting edge of fashion in recent
years. Here's a rundown on the various fibers available.*

NATURAL YARN

Wool provides a natural insulation. It wears forever, and it's wonderfully elastic, responding to your little tugs with its own backward bounce. Wool from Merino sheep is among the softest.

Mohair is a halo of fuzz around a solid core and comes from angora goats. Because it is not so hard-wearing, it frequently is combined with other fibers to make it stronger.

Alpaca yarn is smooth, silky, and extremely warm. It adds softness and a hint of luster when it's blended with wool. Depending on the weight, pure alpaca yarn can be too warm for indoor wear.

Cashmere is the fleece from the cashmere goats of Tibet and China. A little cashmere added to wool or other fibers makes an already-soft yarn exceptionally so.

Angora is soft and fluffy like the rabbit that produces it, but it sheds like crazy and is pricey. Angora frequently is used in combination with other fibers that lessen shedding and strengthen the yarn.

Silk yarn comes from filaments unwound from the cocoons of silkworms. Its lustre adds elegance to other fibers like wool and cotton. Pure silk has no bounce and is difficult for the novice knitter.

Cotton breathes and is absorbent, a natural for warm-weather garments. Cotton lacks the warmth and hard-wearing qualities of wool, and is not so elastic as wool. New blends of cotton and other fibers can make knitting with this yarn more pleasurable than it used to be.

Linen comes from the stem of the flax plant. Linen wicks moisture from the body and grows softer with wear. It adds crispness when blended with cotton or synthetic fibers. Pure linen yarn hangs limp and makes you do all the work. Linen can feel very dry in the hand. It is unforgiving in spotlighting any irregularities in your knitting.

Right
A collection of yarn in varying weights. The pink chunky yarn (center) is far thicker than sport-weight, the yellow yarn on the left.

SYNTHETICS

Forget the scratchy acrylics of yesteryear. Improved synthetics are a big reason we have so many choices in knitting yarn today. They do a good job imitating the look and feel of wool, but they do lack wool's warmth.

In blended yarns, synthetics bring out the best in natural fibers, making them feel lighter and softer in the hand. They are also easier to wash. When used by themselves, acrylic fibers create eye-catching special effects. Microfiber, a very fine acrylic filament, can mimic cashmere. Polyester adds shine and strength to other fibers. and is a mainstay in some novelty yarns.

Rayon is a man-made fiber derived from natural materials. It adds shine and softness and takes dye exceptionally well. However, it has a tendency to stretch.

Nylon, also called polyamide, adds strength to otherwise spongy fibers. Used alone, it can take on different guises, from narrow filaments to fur-like fleece.

Novelty yarns break all the traditional rules. Many of them have thin, solid cores framed by fuzzy haloes or punctuated by "eyelashes," "nubs," "slubs," and even "flags." Some yarns are made from very thin fibers or filaments knit into tubes or double-sided tapes.

Ribbon yarns can be matte or shiny in appearance, wide or narrow, one color, striped, or multi-colored.

Right
Ribbon yarns look both colorful and enchanting when made into modern fashion items.

Chenilles, like velvet to the touch, have been manufactured with extra twist, which makes them difficult to control. They tend to unravel or "worm."

WEIGHTS

Yarns come in a wide range of thicknesses, or weights, from superfine to bulky. In general, thinner yarns call for thinner needles and result in smaller stitches. A lightweight fabric on small needles takes longer to knit than the same-size piece made with bulky yarn and thick needles. Yarns are made by twisting two or more strands (called plies) together to form the yarn. Yarns can be two-ply, three-ply, or four-ply. How thick the yarn is depends as much on how thick and tightly each strand or ply is twisted, as on how many plies the yarn is made from. The number of plies, therefore, does not necessarily indicate the weight of the final yarn. For example, a two-ply yarn, made of tightly twisted thin strands, can be a baby-yarn weight, or, if made of loosely twisted thicker, even fluffy, strands, it can be a bulky-weight yarn.

Fingering or baby yarn is made of two to three very thin strands that have been twisted together. These yarns are used for laces, socks, and baby clothing.

Sport weight yarn, about double the thickness of baby yarn, is used for indoor clothing for all ages.

Worsted weight, a little heavier than sport weight, can be knit up as either indoor or outdoor wear.

Double knitting (DK) is a category the British have that straddles the heavier end of the sport weight yarn and the lighter side of the worsteds.

Chunky and Bulky categories include yarns that are heavier than worsted and that knit up on fat needles in no time at all. The thickest of these fabrics may have great warmth but also can hang stiffly, without much of the flow that comes from good drape.

Yarn selection

The best way to learn about yarns is to look, touch, and knit. As you gain experience in knitting, you will become more confident in your choices.

YARN SUBSTITUTIONS

Sooner or later, you will find reason to substitute your own choice of yarn for the one specified in a pattern. Limit yourself to yarns that behave the same way as the yarn in the design. The instructions were written to fit the yarn, and not the other way around.

A substitute yarn must have the same gauge as the original and share other characteristics with the yarn in the pattern.

Yarns that stretch won't do well with patterns that depend on elastic combinations of knit and purl stitches, like ribbing, as part of the design. Very thick yarns that are super warm may knit up too stiffly to work with patterns that depend on the fabric to hang with any degree of flow, or drape.

The staff in a reputable yarn shop should be able to help you make a good substitution. As well as carrying high quality materials, good shops are unstinting in service. Most likely the person helping you has worked with the yarn you're considering—or someone else in the shop has—and can tell you the advantages and pitfalls of your choice.

When in doubt, you can always buy a single ball of yarn and knit up a sample in the pattern you have chosen.

WORKING WITH YARN

Some yarn comes already wound in balls or skeins that are ready for knitting. Many people like to reach inside, find the yarn end buried in the center, and pull it out. Working from the center out prevents a ball or skein from rolling around every

time you pull on another length of yarn. However, I'm convinced these center ends are conspiring against me. I put the ball in a plastic bag (as shown above) and start with the outer end, then the yarn can roll around inside the bag and it won't matter. The yarn also will stay cleaner and won't get tangled. A zipper across the top of the bag will prevent the yarn from falling out.

Yarn that comes in coils (called hanks) needs winding before it can be used. The most pleasant way to wind yarn is to catch up with a friend while he or she lends assistance. Drape the hank over your friend's arms and start rolling. Or, put the hank over the back of a chair and roll it that way.

YARN SUBSTITUTION EXAMPLE

Say you're making a man's sweater that calls for 22 balls of woolen yarn in white and you want a different yarn with similar characteristics. First check the yardage for the yarn stated in the pattern. Each ball has 86yd (78m) and the pattern calls for 22 balls = a total of 1892yd (86 x 22 = 1892) to complete the pattern.

Your chosen yarn comes in hanks of 153 yards. To work out the number of hanks to buy, divide the total yardage, 1892, by the yardage of one hank, 153.

The result is 12.3, which means you need 13 hanks. I always throw in one extra, just in case, so for this sweater, I would buy 14 hanks.

THE LABEL

Whenever choosing yarn, start with the yarn label. It's a little gold nugget of information. Read it carefully before buying the yarn.

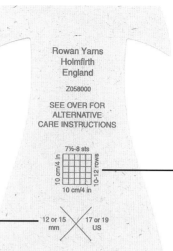

Rowan Yarns
Holmfirth
England

Z058000

SEE OVER FOR
ALTERNATIVE
CARE INSTRUCTIONS

7½-8 sts

10 cm/4 in

10-12 rows

10 cm/4 in

12 or 15 mm   17 or 19 US

Gauge
Gives the number of stitches and rows necessary to knit usually a 4-inch (10cm) square with the recommended size needle. The symbol will tell you the desired size of the finished square.

Recommended needle size
The size expected to produce a specific gauge.

R O W A N

rowan big wool

100% MERINO WOOL
100% MERINO WOLLE
100% MERINO LAINE

Fiber content

100g

In accordance with B.S. 984
Approx Length 80m (87 yds)

www.knitrowan.com

SHADE   LOT

16

5 013712 914850

Weight and yardage
Gives the weight and yardage of each ball. Different yarns packaged in balls of the same weight do not necessarily have the same yardage.

Color
The color number ensures you buy the right shade, especially when the yarn comes in shades similar to each other.

Dye lot
The number on the label identifies a particular batch in which the yarn was dyed. Different dye baths of the same color can produce results which vary noticeably.

Hand wash

Warm iron

Do not bleach

Dry clean in certain solvents

Do not tumble dry
Dry flat out of direct sunlight

Care instructions
How to launder and press the finished item so it does not shrink, stretch, run, or lose color.

A KNITTER'S TOOLS

Here's a guide to the basic tools that are helpful in learning how to knit. As you can see, a pair of knitting needles is just the start!

1. Double-pointed needles
are straight needles with points at both ends. They are used for circular knitting in circumferences too small for a circular needle.

2. Crochet hook
I call this a third hand in knitting because it is useful for a variety of tasks. These hooks come in various sizes. Sizing holes for knitting needles on gauge markers also work for sizing crochet hooks.

3. Point protectors
These fit over the points of needles to prevent stitches from falling off needles when you put the work away.

4. Straight needles
These have a pointed tip at the working end and a knob at the opposite end to prevent stitches from falling off.

5. Tape measure
This is more flexible than a ruler. Use a fiberglass one rather than a fabric one which can stretch.

6. Circular needles
These have points on rigid shafts at each end. The shafts are connected by a thin flexible nylon cable which allows the two working ends to face each other as if they were straight needles.

7. Tapestry needles
These blunt-tipped needles are used to sew seams. They come in several sizes to accommodate various thicknesses of yarn.

8. Stitch holders
These prevent the unraveling of stitches to be worked later in a project. Stitches can also be threaded onto a loop of scrap yarn that is then tied in a knot. Cable needles (not shown) can hold stitches in the front or back of knitting while you work on cables.

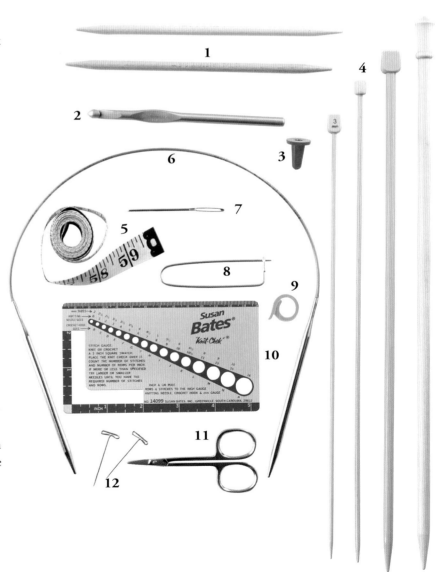

9. Stitch markers

Small plastic rings placed on the needle between stitches, the markers help you keep your place in a pattern without counting. A loop of yarn tied into a knot also can serve as a marker.

10. Gauge markers

This is a metal or plastic ruler that allows you to measure how many stitches you have made for each inch of width in a knitted sample. Some gauge markers feature a vertical ruler that allows you to count the number of rows it takes you to knit an inch in length. Markers also have holes of various sizes to check the diameter of needles.

11. Scissors

Small embroidery scissors with sharp points work best.

12. Pins

Rustproof pins are used for blocking and holding pieces together during seaming

OTHER TOOLS

Bobbins

These are small pieces of plastic with notches that hold limited amounts of yarn for patterns that call for changes in color, thus prevent the yarn from unraveling.

Graph paper

Knitter's graph paper, with rectangles rather than squares, helps you visualize stitch patterns, color changes, and increases and decreases.

Notebook and pencil

Keep a knitting journal to preserve your experiences; keep a record of completed rows or sections.

Row counter

A small counter that slips onto a needle. After each row, you advance the number, thus keeping track of rows in a pattern.

Choosing Needles

There are two basic kinds of knitting needles; straight ones that let you work flat pieces back and forth, and what are known as circular or double-pointed needles that enable you to create seamless pieces by continuously knitting in one direction (*see the next page*). Needles are usually made of plastic or aluminum, although wooden and bamboo needles are popular. Some knitters swear by teflon-coated plastic or nickel-plated brass, saying these finishes allow them to knit faster. This is a personal choice.

The best advice is to knit with whatever feels right for you. Make sure you inspect the needle tips before you buy.

Extra-sharp points can split the yarn. Also, overly dull points can make it difficult for a new knitter to manuever the yarn.

NEEDLE SIZE CHART

Needles come in different sizes according to their diameter. In general, smaller diameter needles are best suited to thinner yarns, although that is not always the case. (Mohair and other fuzzy yarns, for example, need needles of a relatively large diameter.)

Needles are sold according to three sizing systems, depending on the country. The following chart allows you to compare the sizes. The metric system refers to the diameter of the needle.

US	Metric	UK
0	2mm	14
1	2.25mm	13
	2.5mm	
2	2.75	12
	3mm	11
3	3.25mm	10
4	3.5mm	
5	3.75mm	9
6	4mm	8
7	4.5mm	7
8	5mm	6
9	5.5mm	5
10	6mm	4
10½	6.5mm	3
	7mm	2
	7.5mm	1
11	8mm	0
13	9mm	00
15	10mm	000
17	12.75mm	-
19	15mm	-
35	19mm	-

SELECTING THE RIGHT NEEDLE

As you become a little more experienced, you may prefer to use circular or double-pointed instead of regular straight needles. Here's a bit of advice to consider when making your decision.

Most beginners learn on straight needles, which work well on relatively narrow pieces like scarves, some hats, and infant and children's garments. But straight needles frequently cannot hold all the stitches of large projects, like adult-sized sweaters or blankets, unless the stitches are crowded together. As you knit across each row, the growing weight of the piece shifts from one needle to the other row and can make you feel off balance. It is also difficult to measure accurately the length of your knitting when the stitches are crowded together.

Circular needles can be used for back-and-forth knitting and have several advantages over straight needles. They can hold many more stitches than the longest straight needles, allowing you to spread out your work to its intended width before you measure.

Circulars offer more balance, enabling you to rest the knitting in your lap as it grows. They're easy to handle in tight spaces, unlike straight needles, which tend to bump the arms of chairs and poke other people. They are available in different lengths, most commonly from 16" to 36" (40cm to 91.5cm) to accommodate different circumferences. The needle should be smaller than the finished

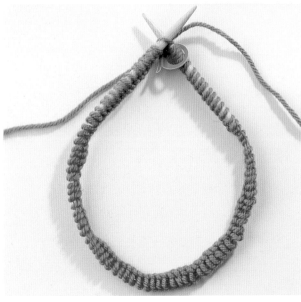

Above
Circular needles are perfect for knitting an item such as a circular hat.

Left
Using a colored stitch marker lets you know when you have come to the end of a round.

circumference of the garment. Sometimes, as a garment narrows for a neckline, you'll have to change to a shorter circular needle or to double-pointed needles.

Circulars shorter than 16 inches (40cm) are awkward to work with. Generally, when the circumference of a knitted item is narrower than 16 inches (40cm)—socks, hats, mittens, and gloves are prime examples—it's time to bring out the double-pointed needles (dpn).

Double-Pointed Needles
These are generally used to knit items (as above) and other, smaller tubular knitted items.

The stitches are cast on to three or four double-pointed needles that are arranged in either a triangle or square. The square formation, with four needles, is easier to handle. In both configurations, an extra needle is used to work the stitches. When that needle is full, the newly emptied needle takes its place as the working needle.

The last cast-on stitch—the one with the working yarn—and the first stitch in the new round—the one on the adjacent needle—can be knitted together for a firmer join. Slip the one on the left needle with the other, and knit the two together.

Newcomers might find the tension wobbles when they knit the first stitch on a double-pointed needle. All of us have ended up with vertical lines of single stitches noticeably bigger than the ones on either side. This can be avoided.

When the working needle is full, keep using it to knit one or two stitches onto the next needle. Then slip the already-knit stitch(es) onto an empty needle and continue.

UNWIND CIRCULAR NEEDLES

Sometimes circular needles that have been curled tightly to fit into packaging just refuse to relax after you get them home. To relax the nylon cable leave it in a bowl of very hot water for 10 minutes or more.

KEEPING EVERYTHING HANDY

A knitting bag should be big enough to hold your entire project and also feature one or more interior pockets for an assortment of tools. You'll need them at unexpected times, and you won't want to go up or down the stairs to get them—or worse yet, have to wait until you get home to do more knitting. Protect the yarn and works-in-progress in plastic that fits inside your project bag.

GET KNITTING

It's time to get the yarn on the needles. Step by step, you'll learn
to make your knitting "grow" before your eyes, secure the
stitches, and assemble pieces into a finished project. Knitting
to fit is also part of the deal in this chapter.

THE CAST-ON

Every knitter develops one or two favorite methods of casting on. Here are two choices that are popular with many knitters. Both methods offer a sturdy edge, as well as flexibility.

Chose one method and practice with it as you learn to knit. Later, when you've mastered the basic techniques, come back and learn the alternative.

Knitting is simply a row of loops on a needle. One by one, each new loop is pulled through the center of the old loop and takes its place on the needle. The old loop, meanwhile, drops down into a permanent place in the fabric. In the very first row, each loop needs a knot at the bottom to stop it from unraveling. The process of creating this foundation row is called "casting on" (CO). The first stitch in casting on is a slip knot.

MAKING A SLIP KNOT

1 Make a loop like the one above, ending with the working end of the yarn over the tail end in an X. Wrap the yarn around the fingers of one hand or make the loop on a flat surface. The working end curls down on the right. The tail, which should be at least 6in (15cm) long, comes from the left.

2 Using a knitting needle or your fingers, pull the working end of the yarn through the center of the first loop. Slide the needle through the new loop.

3 Tighten the new loop by gently pulling the yarn and the yarn end in opposite directions so the knot comes to rest against the needle.

A LONG-TAIL CAST ON

Make the tail at least three times as long as the intended width of the piece you are starting. Add to that at least 8" to 10" (20 to 25cm) for good measure, or more, if you think you might later use the tail to sew up a seam.

Example

If the back of a sweater is to be 20" (51cm) wide, leave at least 60" (153cm), for the tail. Add another 18" (46cm) for sewing up a side seam for a tail that is 78" (195cm) long. When you're done casting on, the excess yarn can be wound up on a bobbin until it's needed.

THUMB (LONG-TAIL) CAST-ON

Thumb Method

The long-tail, or thumb, cast-on uses two strands of yarn, both the tail and the working end that leads to the ball or skein. The only potential pitfall is leaving a tail too short for the number of stitches you need to cast on. But this problem is easily avoided with a rule that works for heavy yarns as well as thinner ones. (*See box on page 24.*)

 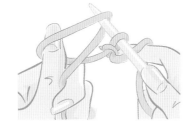

1 Put the slip knot on the right needle so the long tail goes off to the left and the working end is on the right. Wrap the working end over your right index finger and wrap the tail around your left thumb from the palm side of your hand up and over the back of the thumb. Hold the tail in your palm with your fingers.

2 Rotate your left thumb toward your right hand to make a loop of yarn, and then insert the needle through the loop

3 Using your right index finger, guide the working end of the yarn under the tip of the needle from right to left, up the left side, and over the top.

4 With the working strand across the top of the needle, push the tip of the needle and the strand through the center of the loop on your left thumb. Drop the loop from your left thumb. Tighten the tail end into a little knot at the bottom of your new stitch. Repeat the four steps for as many stitches as you need.

DOUBLE-POINTED NEEDLES CAST ON

If you are a beginner knitter, skip this section and go to the knit stitch on page 27.

Working over a table or other flat surface, slip stitches from a conventional needle onto a double-pointed needle.

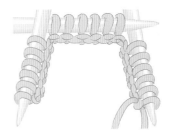

1 Arrange stitches equally on three or four double-pointed needles in either a triangle or a square.

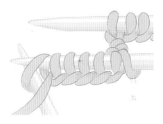

2 In both forms, the extra needle works the stitches. When that needle is full, the newly emptied needle becomes the working needle.

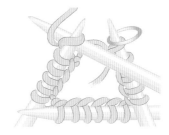

3 Arrange the stitches so the knotted bottoms are in the center of the formation. Add a marker.

CABLE CAST-ON

The cable cast-on doesn't depend on a long tail. It has a beautiful edge and is very hard wearing; perfect for ribbed cuffs of sleeves. At the same time, it retains the elasticity that ribbed edges need. For this method, use two knitting needles

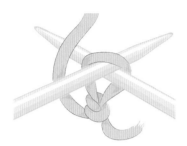

1 Leaving a tail, make a slipknot and put it on a needle. With your right hand, insert the tip of a second needle through the middle of the loop on the left needle. Make sure the tip of the right needle goes under the left needle.

Wrap the working end of the yarn up the left side and across the top of the right needle. This is your new stitch-in-the-making.

2 With the right needle, draw the new loop through the original one on the left needle. Don't drop the first loop. Instead, move the point of the left needle across the front of the new loop just past its right edge. Slip the new stitch onto the left needle as shown. Draw the new loop closed, but not tight, around the left needle.

3 Insert the right needle between the two loops on the left needle. Make sure the right needle is under the left needle in an X position. Wrap the working yarn from under and around the right needle as before. This is the newest stitch-in-the-making.

4 Draw the loop on the right needle under the left needle and toward you through the space between the two stitches. The loop is free on the right needle. Transfer it to the left needle as before. Leave the yarn loose enough that the right needle can get inbetween the last two stitches. Repeat the last two steps until you have the desired number of stitches.

Above
No matter what the pattern of your knitted project—in garter stitch (photographed at the top) or in extra-wide ribbing (photographed above)—a neat edge is dependent on the stitches being cast on evenly.

THE KNIT STITCH

The knit stitch (k) is a series of motions, the basic dance step for a repertoire with countless variations. To get your bearings, understand that the stitches you have cast on are lined up like a chorus line facing left. The left "arms" of the loops are closest to you. These left arms or front sections are called front loops and the back sections are called back loops.

1 The needle with the cast-on stitches goes in the left hand. In all except the first stitch, only the front loops (or left arms) are visible.

Bring the tip of the right needle to the left of the first loop on the left needle. Insert the needle through the center of the loop, pushing the right needle tip away from you.

2 The right needle has opened up the first stitch on the left needle and has begun turning it to face you. Note that the right and left needles form an x inside the loop, with the right needle under the left one.

3 To form a new loop, wrap the yarn under the right needle from right to left, up over the top and toward the right again.

4 With the right needle, draw the new loop out of the X formation. In this motion, the right needle passes under the left needle and comes up.

The Finish

You're not finished until you slip the old loop off the left needle. Move the right needle to the right until the old loop directly beneath the new stitch falls off the tip of the left needle. This loop has made a quarter turn and now faces you squarely.

As you work the stitches from the left needle, you need to push the remaining stitches into working position near the tip of the left needle, but move just a few stitches at a time to keep them from accidentally falling off the needle before they are worked. When all the stitches have been knitted onto the right needle, you have completed one row. Turn the right needle around and place it in the left hand, ready to begin a new row. To start each knit row, begin with the working yarn held behind the needle.

THE PURL STITCH

You're on your way to understanding the purl stitch (p) if you remember that it is the reverse of the knit stitch. For example, the front of the knit stitch is smooth and the front of the purl stitch is bumpy. Remember that the yarn always must hang in back at the start of the knit stitch. It must always hang in front at the beginning of a purl stitch.

In knitting, the words "back" and "front" are used in relation to you, the knitter. Purl stitches are often made on the "wrong" or "reverse" side of your knitting, But as long as you work a row with the bumpy purl stitches facing you, they make up the "front" of your work.

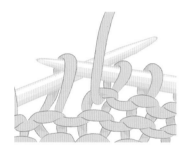

1 Insert the tip of the right needle from right to left in the first stitch on the left needle. The two needles form an X inside the loop, with the right needle in front.

2 Pick up the working yarn from its starting position in front and wrap it counter clockwise around the right needle, (that is, back over the top of the needle, bringing it forward under the needle).

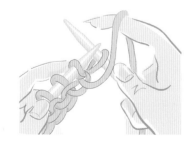

3 Move the right needle and the new loop backwards out of the X and through the old loop. Note that the motion finishes with the right needle in back of the left one.

4 Push the loop off the left needle and repeat the purling motions for as many stitches as you need.

Pulling Through
For many people, the motion described in Step 3 poses a particular challenge. Good tension on the working yarn helps keep the new loop in place on the right needle. As the right needle backs out of the X, and goes under the left needle, it might help to brace the tip of the right needle against the shaft of the left needle. Some people might need a counterclockwise twist of the right hand to bring the new loop up behind the left needle.

HOLDING THE YARN

Holding the needles and yarn in a consistent way helps get even tension on the working strand so that the stitches come out the same size. The thing that matters most is that holding the yarn is comfortable and effective for you.

THE ENGLISH METHOD

This is probably the most commonly used in the United States and Britain.

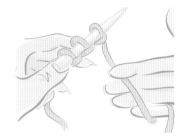
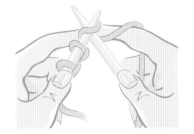

1 Hold the thumb and fingers of your left hand over one needle like a tent, so that the fingers can work together. With the right hand, wrap the working end of the yarn around the little finger, under the hand and up and over the index finger.

2 With both the hands tented over the pointed end of the needles, the right index finger wraps the yarn and controls the tension.

THE CONTINENTAL METHOD

In the Continental method, common in Europe, the yarn is held in the left hand.

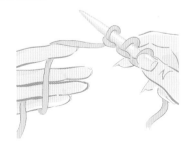

1 This hold is the mirror image of the English method. Wrap the working yarn over the little finger on your left hand, under the hand, and over the left index finger.

2 When hands and needles work together, the right hand controls the working needle and the left index finger controls the tension.

Holding two yarns
When using two yarns, be sure to keep them from tangling. Try keeping each ball in a separate bag.

KNIT & PURL STITCH LIBRARY

Here are several combinations of knit and purl stitches that form the backbone of the knitting repertoire. They show up in many basic patterns as well as designs requiring advanced skills.

PLACING THE YARN

Before you knit, the working yarn must be in the back of the work. Before you can purl, the yarn must hang in front. When you alternate between knit and purl in the same row, don't forget to move the yarn under the needles to the correct starting position before working the next stitch.

Yarn at back

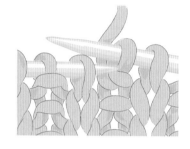

The yarn is at the back of the needle, ready to knit.

Yarn at front

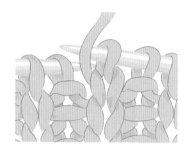

The yarn is at the front of the needle, ready to purl.

Garter stitch
Knit every row.

Stockinette stitch
Row 1: Right side, knit.
Row 2: Wrong side, purl.
Repeat rows 1 and 2.

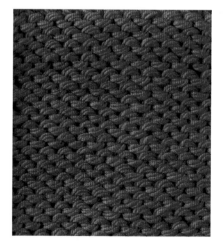

Reverse stockinette stitch
Row 1: Right side, purl.
Row 2: Wrong side, knit.
Repeat rows 1 and 2.

Seed stitch

Over an odd number of stitches:
Row 1: Knit 1, *purl 1, knit 1,
repeat from * until end of row.
Turn work. Repeat row 1.
Over an even number of stitches:
Row 1: *Knit 1, purl 1, repeat from
* until end of row.
Row 2: *Purl 1, knit 1, repeat from
* until end of row.

Double seed (Moss) stitch

For an even number of stitches
Row 1 (right side): *Knit one, purl
one, repeat from * to end.
Row 2: Repeat row 1.
Row 3: *Purl one, knit one, repeat
from * to end.
Row 4: Repeat row 3.
Repeat rows 1 through 4.

RIBBING

Ribbing provides an elastic edge to sleeves, necklines, and the bottoms of
sweaters and other garments. It can also be a design feature. There are
many types of ribbing, just as there are many combinations of knit and
purl. Here are just two of them.

Left
Knit 1, purl 1 ribbing
Over an even number of stitches:
Row 1: *Knit 1, purl 1, repeat
from * to end. Row 2: *Purl 1,
Knit 1, repeat from * to end.
Repeat these two rows.
Over an odd number of stitches:
Row 1: Knit 1, *purl 1, knit 1,
repeat from * to end. Turn work.
Row 2: Purl 1, *knit 1, purl 1,
repeat from * to end. Repeat these
two rows.

Above
Knit 2, purl 2 ribbing
Multiple of 4 stitches, plus two
extra for symmetry.
Row 1: Knit 2, *purl 2, knit 2,
repeat from * to end.
Row 2: Purl 2, *knit 2, purl 2,
repeat from * to end.
Repeat these two rows.

BINDING OFF

Binding off (BO, sometimes called casting off, CO) is the end game in a piece of knitting. It reminds me of leap frog in that each stitch jumps over the one in front of it and gets locked into place.

FASTENING OFF
If you are binding off to finish a piece, bind off until all the stitches are gone but the last one on the right needle. Cut the yarn, leaving a long tail. Remove the needle from the last stitch and draw the yarn end through the loop of this last stitch. Pull the end to tighten it and stop your work from unraveling. This process is called fastening off.

Knit Bind-off

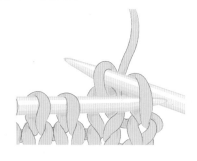

I Knit two stitches. Insert the tip of the left needle into the front of the stitch on the right needle that was knitted first.

2 Lift this stitch over the other stitch and drop it off the tip of the needle. One stitch has been bound off and one stitch remains on the right needle.

3 Knit another stitch and repeat the "leapfrog" motion to bind off each stitch until you have bound off as many stitches as needed.

Purl bind-off

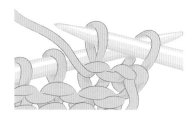

I Purl two stitches. Insert the tip of the left needle into the front of the stitch on the right needle that was knitted first.

2 Lift this stitch over the other one and drop it off the tip of the right needle.

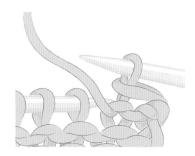

3 Purl another stitch and repeat the "leapfrog" motion to bind off each stitch until you have bound off as many stitches as needed. If you are finishing this piece, fasten off as for the knit bind-off (*see above*).

SHAPING

Learning to shape your knitting will greatly expand your choice of projects and boost your confidence as well. Most shaping involves increasing (inc) or decreasing (dec) the number of stitches on your knitting needles.

INCREASES

Increasing techniques are variations on knit and purl stitches. Some are all-purpose methods, others are chosen for their decorative effect, or for their ability to hide among the other stitches.

Increases are used, for example, to widen the sleeves of sweaters as they approach the armholes, and to widen the bottoms of sweaters after the ribbing has been completed.

Most increases are made on the front side so you can see how they will look in the finished fabric. Some increases ask you to work through the front or back of a loop and assume you're facing the length of the needle squarely. The front is the side nearer to you, and the back is farther away, whether the stitch is a knit or purl, or whether you're working on the right side or the wrong side of the pattern. When you look at a needle, the stitches for knitting always faces left: the working needle approaches the front of a stitch from the left and the back of a stitch from the right.

A pattern may or may not specify a particular type of increase, but ultimately you, the knitter, get to choose which method suits your knitting style.

Make One

M1 puts the increase in the strand between two stitches. This technique makes a nearly invisible increase on the front side of stockinette stitch.

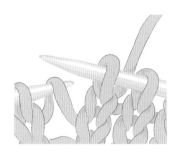 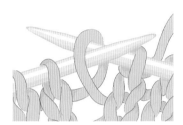

1 Insert the tip of the left needle from front to back under the horizontal strand between the first stitch on the left needle and the first one on the right needle.

2 Insert the tip of the right needle through the raised strand, sliding the right needle behind the left needle. The motion twists the raised bar into a loop. Knit into the back of the loop and remove the left needle. One new stitch has been created on the right needle.

The Bar Increase

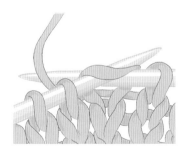 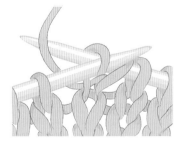

1 Knit one stitch to the point where the new loop is on the right needle, but don't drop the old stitch from the left needle.

2 Insert the tip of the right needle through the old loop, with the right needle sliding behind the left. Wrap the yarn for a knit stitch and pull it through. Drop the old stitch from the left needle. Two stitches have been worked in one stitch.

The Yarn Over

The yarn over (yo) is versatile. It creates an eyelet in the process of making a new stitch and is a mainstay of openwork patterns. Often, the eyelet is desired but the increase is not. Then, the yarn over is preceded or followed by a decrease.

Yarn Over Between Knit Stitches

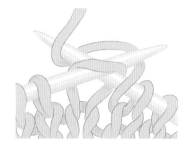

Bring the yarn forward between the right and left needles. Wrap the yarn over the top of the right needle to the back again and knit the first stitch on the left needle.

Yarn Over Between Purl Stitches

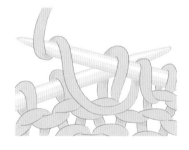

The working yarn hangs in front before a purl stitch. Lift it up over the right needle to the back and bring it under the right needle to the front again. Make a purl stitch in the first loop on the left needle.

The Lifted Increase

The lifted increase is not universally known, but it has the advantage of being nearly invisible in almost any situation.

Right Slanting

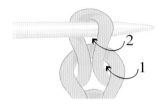

1 In the row below the loop on the left needle, knit into right side of the stitch. Don't knit through the center of the stitch. The correct entry point is shown by arrow number 1. With the just-made stitch on the right needle, raise the right needle one row. Make a knit stitch at arrow number 2, through the first loop on the left needle.

Left Slanting

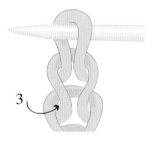

2 The entry point for the right needle is marked by arrow number 3. Note that the stitch is two rows below the first loop on your right needle. To get the left side of that stitch into position for the increase, insert the tip of the left needle from back to front. Remember, it goes through the left side, not the center of the stitch. Lift up the loop on the left needle, and insert the right needle for the knit stitch.

DECREASES

Gradually decreasing the number of stitches is the mainstay of shaping armholes and necklines of sweaters and the crowns of hats. Decreases may be put at the edges of the work, where seams will cover them. But the decreases result in an irregular edge that can make seaming more difficult. Decreases placed a few stitches away from the edges can become a design element. This kind of shaping is called full-fashioned. Full-fashioned shaping leaves uniform-edge stitches for faster seaming.

Basic Right-Slanting Decrease

Knit two together (k2tog)

1 Insert the right needle from left to right through the center of the next two stitches on the left needle. Wrap the yarn as usual for a knit stitch. Pull the new loop through both stitches on the left needle. Drop those two stitches from the left needle and your decrease is complete.

Basic Left-Slanting Decreases

SSK (not illustrated)
Slip one, slip one, knit two together

Here's a left-slanting decrease that doesn't twist stitches.

Insert the right needle in the first stitch on the left needle as if to knit (knitwise) and merely transfer it to the right needle without knitting it. Slip the next stitch on the needle knitwise, the same way as for the first. Don't try to slip both stitches at the same time, or it will affect the look of the finished increase.

Insert the left needle into the front sides of the loops just slipped. The left needle should be in front of the right needle. Knit both these two stitches together.

Slip 1, knit 1, pass slip stitch over (not illustrated)
(sl 1, k1, psso; also called skp)

This decrease looks like the SSK decrease, but it is worked in a different way. Insert the right needle in the first stitch on the left needle as if to knit (knitwise) and transfer it to the right needle without knitting it. Knit the next stitch from the left needle. Then lift the slipped stitch over this knitted stitch (as if you were binding off) and drop it, leaving only the one knitted stitch on the left needle.

Right
Necklines such as this soft roll neck, and sleeves, are defined using increases and decreases.

Knit two together through the back loops (k2tog tbl)

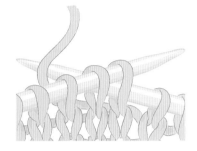

I Insert the right needle from right to left through the center of the first two stitches on the left needle. The right needle should slide behind the left needle and the backs of the two loops hug the back of the right needle.

Make a knit stitch, pulling the new loop through both stitches on the left needle. Drop the two stitches from the left needle and the decrease is done. This decrease produces a twisted stitch.

Purl Decreases

Purl two together
(p2tog)

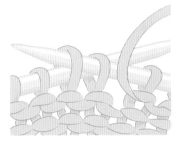

I Insert the right needle from right to left through the fronts of the first two stitches on the left needle. Make a purl stitch and draw the new stitch through both loops on the left needle. Drop the two loops from the left needle to finish the decrease. This decrease slants to the right.

Purl two together through back loop (p2tog tbl)

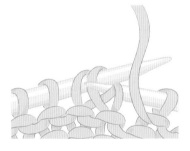

I Angle the right needle from back to front. Insert the tip of the right needle through the back of the second stitch on the left needle and then the back of the first stitch. The movement twists both stitches. Purl one and drop the two stitches from the left needle. This decrease slants to the left.

THE STITCH GAUGE

The stitch gauge is the number of stitches it takes to cover a certain width. The gauge is frequently expressed over a width of four inches (10 centimeters). For example, for one chunky yarn is 12 stitches over four inches (10 centimeters).

The row gauge is the number of rows needed to knit a particular length. The success of a project depends on your knitting to the gauge the pattern requires.

Knitting a sample, called a swatch, is probably the last thing you want to do when you are itching to start right in. Slow yourself down and do it. If your stitches are too big or too small, your new sweater will fit either a small elephant or a large child, but not you. Your enthusiasm will turn to disappointment and I'd hate to see you turn off knitting because you didn't make the sample. Think of the sample as the start of something wonderful.

The swatch should be at least 4" (10cm) wide and 4" (10cm) long, to compensate for variations in hand-knit stitches. You'll get a more accurate count by working swatch squares of 6" or even 8" (15cm or 20cm).

Work your swatch in stockinette stitch (knit one row, purl one row) unless the garment calls for other stitch patterns.

When there is more than one stitch pattern or a change in color, you can work all the variations together in one big swatch. Various combinations of knit and purl stitches affect the length and width of the overall fabric in different ways. Reserve a couple of stitches on each side of the swatch for knitting in every row, no matter what the stitch in the remainder of the row. This kind of border

(selvage) will prevent the sides from curling.

When the swatch is finished, don't bind off the stitches. Put them on a roomy stitch holder so they do not crowd together, or thread a tapestry needle with a generous length of scrap yarn and run it through the loops. Tie the ends of scrap yarn into a knot so the stitches on the swatch don't unravel. Lay the swatch on a flat surface without stretching it or bunching it up.

Measure the width and length of the sample, using a metal, fiberglass or plastic ruler. (Cloth tapes can stretch and give you inaccurate results.) Count the number of stitches in the width and the number of rows in the

Below
Measuring length for row count.

Below
Measuring width for stitch count.

Below
Measuring length and width count with a stitch measure.

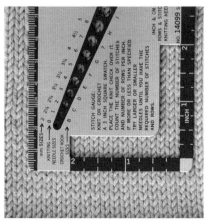

length of the sample and jot the numbers down. To get the gauge for one square inch, divide the total number of stitches by the width of your swatch and the total number of rows by the length.

Once you have the number of stitches and rows for 1"(2.5cm), you can multiply by 4 to see if your gauge matches the pattern.

For example, I've knit a swatch in garter stitch with 26 stitches on size 11 needles that is 8½" (22cm) wide. That means the stitch gauge, for 1", is 26 stitches divided by 8½" (22cm), or 3¼" (8cm). Over 4" (10cm) the gauge is 3.25 stitches multiplied by 4" (10 cm) = 13.

My sample is 8inches long and has 47 rows. The row gauge, per inch, is 47 rows divided by 8 inches (20 cm) or 5.9 rows per inch. The row gauge over four inches (10 cm) is 5.9 rows multiplied by 4 inches (10 cm), or 23.6 rows.

Most patterns give row and stitch gauges in whole numbers. It's acceptable to be a small fraction off on row or stitch gauge if your entire sample is four square inches or larger, preferably larger. But be aware that the small error becomes magnified when it is applied to a garment that is much wider and longer than your swatch. Row gauge is especially important in sweater sleeves, when directions call for stitch increases according to intervals measured in rows.

If you don't have enough stitches or rows to match the project gauge, switch to smaller sized needles. If you have too many stitches or rows, use larger-sized needles. The recommended needle

size in the directions and on the yarn wrapper is just that—a recommendation, not a mandate. Everyone knits differently.

Having said that, if you can't get a gauge that comes even close to the one in the pattern, it's a sure sign that you need to pick a different yarn.

Sometimes, especially when I'm knitting in stockinette stitch with wool on medium or small-sized needles, I've gone right from the swatch to the project and have had no problems with size. It is a good idea to check your gauge as your project progresses to be sure you are maintaining the proper tension.

Above
The same yarn knitted on different needle sizes, can result in stitches that vary greatly in size, affecting gauge dramatically. Here, a double-knit weight yarn, knitted on size 3 (3.25mm) needles, produced a dense fabric.

Above
Here is the same double-knit yarn worked up on size 10 (6mm) needles and as you can see the stitch pattern is larger and there are fewer stitches to each inch (centimeter).

READING THE PATTERN

The pattern is the starting point for turning your vision into reality. It's one thing to see a photo of a sweater you must have. It's quite another thing to be able to touch it and wear it. The pattern leads you toward that moment.

The most important aspect of the pattern in predicting success is the one often ignored—gauge. It is important to remember that point. However, having explained that in detail on the previous pages, here is a breakdown of the other important information you need to understand in the pattern. You will discover:

- A description of the style of the garment and whether it should be roomy or fit close to the body
- Specific measurements for various sizes
- A list of materials and tools
- Separate directions for pattern stitches

Most patterns include schematics of the various pieces along with measurements for length and width at various points in each piece. Patterns that call for two identical pieces or pieces that are mirror images of each other, like two fronts of a cardigan sweater, show only one diagram to represent both.

More and more new patterns come with a bar logo giving knitters an idea of the skill-level needed to complete the project, although the interpretation of terms like "beginner," "easy," "advanced beginner," and "intermediate" inevitably are subjective.

To the uninitiated, knitting directions may look like an arcane language of abbreviations. Knitters learn many of them, one by one, as they practice new skills. If there's an unfamiliar term, consult the glossary on page 56, or ask an experienced friend.

Make a photocopy of the pattern so you can carry it in your knitting bag without lugging around the weight of a magazine or book. A single copy for personal use does not violate any copyright laws.

Step-by-step directions for various sizes include sets of numbers crammed together inside pairs of parentheses. For example, cast on 80 (85, 90, 95) means cast on 80 sts for the smallest size. The numbers within the parenthesis indicate the number of sts for each progressively larger size, ending with 95 sts for the largest size.

Make sure the size you are making jumps out at you by highlighting or circling the correct number. The numbers for various sizes are given in the same sequence all the way through the instructions. If only one number is given at a particular step, it applies to all sizes.

Above
Row gauge is critical when knitting something such as this poncho to a flattering length.

THE FIT

Knitting a swatch for gauge will tell you whether the project will come out the intended size, but is that size for you?

Will that style look good on you?

Look at the photo that accompanies a pattern the same way you would size up a garment on the rack before deciding whether to try it on. Is it shaped at the waist? And is your waist one of your good features? How far below the waist will the sweater hang? Will it hit the hips at the wrong place? And what about the collar? Does it flatter your face, or accentuate imperfections?

Sized to Fit

Once you're satisfied with the style, turn your attention to fit. The words "small", "medium", and "large" can be misleading when it comes to selecting a pattern size.

Some clues come from the finished measurements of the garment. Key statistics—the circumference of the bust or chest at the underarms and the length of the garment—are listed near the beginning of the instructions.

Complete sets of measurements for various pieces of the pattern are noted along the borders of diagrams at the end of the instructions, with larger sizes in parentheses. To see how the

Left
To make sure the armhole is comfortable and does not gape, check the length of the pattern from armhole to shoulder against your armhole depth.

garment will fit, compare the finished measurements to your actual body measurements. You will not be any happy if, after all that work, the sweater doesn't fit your shape and size. This is no time for vanity.

Several measurements are necessary to evaluate the pattern you have chosen. For the sake of accuracy, don't try to take your own measurements. Have a friend do it (and swear her to secrecy).

MEASURING

Use a measuring tape you are sure has not stretched. Check it by lining it up against a metal or plastic ruler.

Take measurements snugly, without any room between the body and the tape. On the other hand, don't pull the tape so tightly that it digs in to the body.

THE BODY MEASUREMENTS

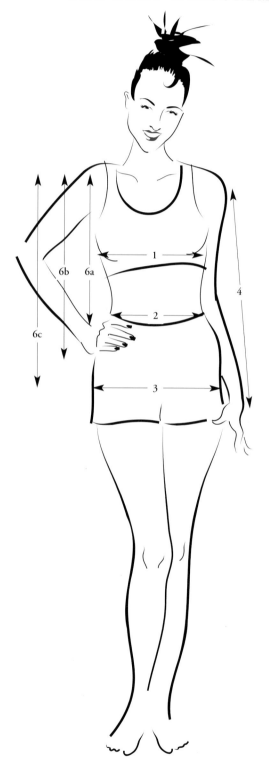

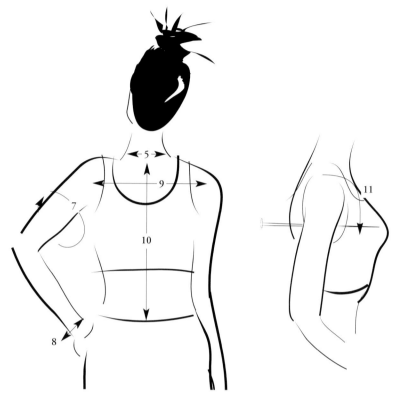

1. **Bust or chest**   Measure around the fullest part.
2. **Waist**   Measure around the narrowest part of the torso. Important for garments shaped at the sides.
3. **Full Hip**   Measure the widest part of the hip and bottom.
4. **Sleeve length**   For long fitted sleeves, measure from the tip of the shoulder bone to the wrist bone. For short sleeves, measure from the tip of the shoulder bone to the desired length. For drop-shouldered sleeves with no sleeve cap, measure from the underarm to the wrist bone.
5. **Neck width**   This is an approximate measurement, taken from the back, to make sure the pattern leaves enough of a neck opening.
6. **Finished length**   Cropped—waist length.
   High hip—generally 3" to 4" below waist.
   Full hip—generally 7" to 9" below waist.
7. **Upper arm**   Measure around fullest part of the upper arm. This measurement can be helpful in evaluating garments designed to be close fitting.
8. **Wrist**   Make sure the cuffs on the sleeves are wide enough.
9. **Shoulders**   Measure the width of the shoulder bone across the back, from one tip to another. This number helps determine whether sleeveless tops and fitted sleeves will fall where you want them.
10. **Neck to waist**   Measure from the bone at the bottom of the neck to the waist.
11. **Armhole**   Measure the depth of the armhole from the tip of the shoulder bone to a ruler or other straight edge held under the arm.

CATEGORIES OF EASE FOR FIT

Very-close fitting   Actual chest or bust measurements or less

Close-fitting   Chest/bust measurement plus 1" to 2" (2.5cm to 5cm) extra

Standard-fitting   Chest/bust measurement plus 2" to 4" (5cm to 10cm)

Loose-fitting   Chest/bust measurement plus 4" to 6" (10cm to 15cm)

Oversized   Chest/bust measurement plus 6" (15cm) or more

Below
This sweater has sufficient ease to allow for a couple of layers under it, and the length allows a man to reach into his back pocket easily. The other measurements to get right here are the width of the neck, and the length of each sleeve.

Finished garment measurements
When figuring length, the finished measurements are the same as actual body measurements. When figuring circumference, the finished measurements are almost always larger than actual body measurements to account for ease. There are several categories for ease (*see chart above*).

When you look at the diagrams in a pattern, bear in mind that the width of the back of a sweater is half the circumference of a pullover or a buttoned cardigan.

Generally, finished bust measurements are used as the main guide for selecting the size to make. But if the garment falls to the hip and that measurement is larger than the bust, it is the hip number that should guide the choice of size. The overall length of sweaters can easily be adjusted below the armholes. The length of sleeves can be adjusted below the armhole.

A shortcut to figuring fit is to compare the finished measurements in a knitting pattern with a comfortable sweater of a similar style that is already in your closet. This shortcut could work well in determining the sleeve length from underarm to wrist.

However, comparing the pattern's finished measurements to a completed garment will not be as accurate as working with the actual body measurements.

THE
FINISHING
TOUCH

The garment is off the needles, the yarn

balls have shrunk to but a few

strands,and you feel a sense of relief.

However, there is more to do.

The garment must be finished with you

paying as much attention to the

finishing details as you did to the

knitting. The finish

work takes time and patience,

but you will be rewarded

with a perfect knitted garment.

BLOCKING

The way a handknit sweater is put together can make it into an heirloom or something that was "homemade." Smoothing out the stitches, making seams disappear, and other other details deserve as much attention as the knitting and purling.

When the knitting comes off the needles, it's not quite finished. It needs blocking to set the final dimensions of the piece, even out the stitches, and smooth the knitted surface.

Blocking is done with water or steam in several different ways, depending on the fiber. Some synthetics cannot be blocked at all. Check the yarn label to find the maker's recommendations.

For me, the biggest challenge in blocking has not been the process itself but finding a padded surface that can remain undisturbed while a wet piece of knitting dries flat in its own time. For years I set up temporary blocking boards by taping layers of toweling to scrap lumber, a tedious job in itself. Recently I discovered homasote, a thick fiberboard made of recycled paper that is absorbent, holds pins well, and is not damaged by the amount of water used in blocking knitting.

Cork would also work as a blocking board, but it is expensive. Some people prefer to use sheets of styrofoam insulation. Others use carpets or rugs.

To block knitting made of wool, cotton, and most other natural fibers, wet the piece thoroughly and roll it up in terry towels to take

out the excess moisture. Lay it flat on your blocking board, right side up, and pat it into the desired measurements, working from the numbers on the diagrams in your pattern. Pin down the edges with strong, rust-proof pins. (I like tailor's pins, or T pins, which are easy to grasp and can be pushed into the blocking board with a little force.) A blocking board cover made of gingham fabric in one-inch checks can serve as a measuring guide.

After the knitting has dried, the piece has gained a smooth, finished surface and a crisp outline.

Synthetics, as well as natural fibers like mohair and angora, can be pinned to the blocking board while they are still dry and then dampened with a spray bottle.

Steaming can take the place of wet blocking as long as the iron is used with extreme care. The iron

Above
Here, the evening bag project knitted with a gold yarn (*see page 84*) is pinned to a piece if gingham on a blocking board to ensure that it dries to the shape required.

should hover just above the knitted fabric and never rest on it. Don't use heat on most acrylics, or if you do, the heat should be turned down to prevent the acrylic from melting. When you're not sure how to treat a particular yarn, check the cleaning directions on the yarn label for safety's sake.

SEAMING

With some time and very little effort, you can create seams that are invisible, or nearly so, along most edges of your knitting. From a distance, it's easy to see where to put a seam, but I sometimes wander off track when I'm focusing on one or two stitches, especially in a tight space. In these cases, I've learned that it takes less time to baste the path of the needle with thin scrap yarn in a contrasting color. The basting stitches are pulled out when the seam is done.

The most common of these invisible seams is called the mattress stitch. It runs vertically, picking up the horizontal bars between the edge and second stitches on each piece.

Below
Sleeves must be carefully fitted into the armhole on the main body.

Beginning a seam

Lay the pieces right side up next to each other. Thread a tapestry needle with matching yarn or with a long tail from a cast-on row and begin at the end of the seam.

    With the yarn attached to one piece, pull the needle from the back to front through the bottom edge stitch on the opposite piece. Return to the first piece, and again insert the needle from back to front through the bottom edge stitch. Draw the two pieces together.

Mattress stitch on stockinette stitch

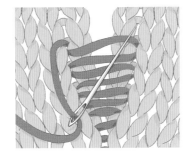

Once the two pieces have been joined at the bottom, find the horizontal bar between the first selvage and the second stitch on the piece opposite the one where the yarn last emerged. Cross over and pull the needle under that horizontal bar. Then return to the other piece and pull the needle under the matching bar. Sew from side to side in this fashion, matching the bars and drawing the two selvage pieces together.

An invisible seam on garter stitch

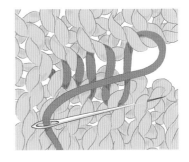

As with the stockinette stitch, the vertical edges of two garter stitch pieces are lined up together, right side up. Instead of picking up the bar between two stitches, pull the needle through the edge stitches themselves. Pick up the bottom bump on a garter ridge on one side, and the top bump of the corresponding ridge on the other side. Keep alternating the top and bottom bumps on the garter ridges as you work your way up the seam.

Invisible horizontal seam
Joining 2 cast-off edges

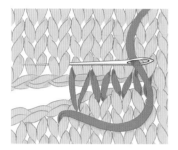

This seam is used to join two cast-off edges, such as shoulder seams, that line up horizontally stitch for stitch. Pull the needle and yarn from side to side under a stitch at the edge of one piece. On the opposite piece, shown on the bottom of the illustration, insert the needle in the center of the corresponding stitch and pull it through to the surface in the center of the next stitch.

Invisible vertical to horizontal

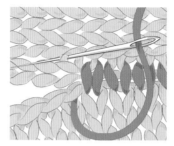

This seam, also called stitches-to-rows seam, is used to sew the bound-off edge of a sleeve cap to the vertical line of an armhole.

Line up the top of the sleeve perpendicular to the armhole edge. Pull a needle and thread through the center of a stitch on top row of sleeve. On the opposite side, run the needle behind a bar connecting the first and second stitches. Sometimes you must catch two bars at once, because there are usually more rows at the armhole edge than there are stitches across the top of the sleeve. On the sleeve side, push needle back through center of the stitch where it last emerged and pull it up through the center of the next sleeve stitch.

Backstitch

The backstitch is a strong seam that can take some stress. It can also be used to take in fullness, although any seam allowance should not exceed ⅜". As a guide, run a basting thread in contrasting yarn along seamline of each piece.

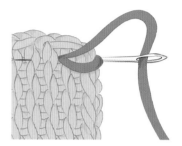

1. Place the pieces right sides together and pin in place. Wrap the yarn around the ends of the pieces twice, pulling the needle through the fabric from back to front. The needle should emerge about ¼" forward of the first wrap.

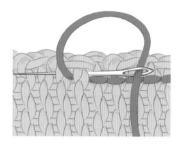

2. Push the needle back through where the yarn emerged and surface it about ¼" beyond the point where it came through the second time. Continue, moving 1 step back and 2 steps forward, in a straight line.

Joining ribbed edges

These are variations on the invisible mattress stitch, right side up.

Two knit stitch edges

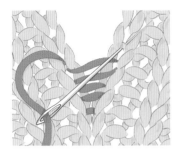

Instead of using the horizontal bars between two stitches, catch the horizontal bars in the center of the knit stitch at the edge of each piece. Pull the sewing needle under the bar at the center of the knit stitch on one side and then do the same in the center of the corresponding knit stitch on the other side.

Two purl-stitch edges

Ignore the purl stitches at the edges. Instead, neatly work the seam through the horizontal bars in the center of the adjacent knit stitches.

Overcasting

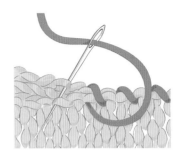

This seam is usually done on the wrong side. Put the right sides together, lining up rows evenly. Pull the needle and yarn through the strands at the edges of the pieces. Repeat the back-to-front stitch motion. them up evenly. Overcasting can also turn into a design element when done on the right side.

Seaming a Slip Stitch Edge

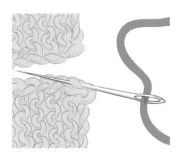

1. With right sides facing, put needle under the outer edge of the slip stitch and bring it up through the center of that loop.

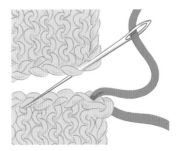

2. Move to the corresponding stitch on the opposite side. The illustration shows the needle moving from top to bottom of the outer edge of the slip stitch. Before drawing the yarn through insert the needle from the bottom to top in the next slip stitch. Cross to the other side and repeat.

How to weave in ends

Above is an example of ends neatly woven into the fabric. To do this, thread a tail into a tapestry needle, and bring it to the wrong side of the knitting. Sew the tail in and out of the garter bumps for about 1½" (3.75cm). Turn and work in the opposite direction for about 1" (2.5cm). Trim the tail.

PICKING UP STITCHES AT THE EDGE

The shape of borders, necklines, and collars often begins with new stitches that "grow" out of the edges of finished pieces.

Because the stitches should make a neat, even line, I usually baste along the path where I plan to pick up. The work is done right side up, so the emerging line of stitches is clearly visible.

Some people use a knitting needle to pick up the stitches, but you might find a crochet hook is easier to manipulate. I think it does a neater job. I don't mind the extra step of sliding each new loop from the crochet hook to a knitting needle. (This could, however, make a neck tighter than it ought to be, so be careful when working around a neckline.)

The crochet hook and knitting needle should be about two sizes smaller than the size you would use to actually work the stitches.

Circular knitting needles will work better than straight ones in receiving the picked-up stitches, especially on curved edges. Once the stitches have been picked up, change needle size to start knitting.

Picking up along a shaped edge
On a neckline or other shaped edge, it's important to pick up stitches in a neat line. The neckline is a focal point of the sweater. Also the picked-up stitches often hide an irregular raw edge. Avoid drawing the new loops through any holes that may have resulted from shaping. Instead, put your crochet hook through a nearby firm stitch so the picked-up stitch hides the hole (see *illustrations*).

PICKING UP ALONG A HORIZONTAL EDGE

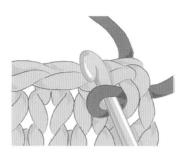 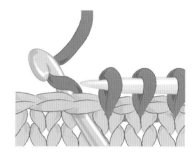

1 Draw a loop of yarn from back to front, using a crochet hook inserted through the center of a stitch just below the bound-off edge.

2 Slide the loop onto a knitting needle so that the back of the loop leads to the working yarn. Otherwise the stitch will be twisted. Be careful not to stretch the loop or to make a hole in the finished fabric.

PICKING UP ALONG A VERTICAL EDGE

 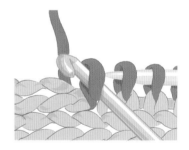

1 Beginning at the corner of the fabric, draw the yarn through the channel between the edge stitch and the next one.

2 Slide the new stitch onto a knitting needle so that the back of the loop leads to the ball of yarn.

If you pick up one stitch for every row on the vertical edge, you will have too many stitches. Because each stitch is wider than each row is tall, the work will start to ripple.

To figure out how many stitches to pick up on a vertical edge, go back to your gauge and calculate the ratio of stitches to rows.

For example, if you are getting 12 stitches and 16 rows over a 4" (10 cm) square, it's equivalent to three stitches and four rows per inch. The ratio means you should pick up three stitches over every four rows on a vertical edge. Pick up one stitch in each of three consecutive rows, then skip one row.

PICKING UP ALONG A SHAPED EDGE

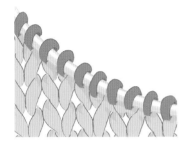

1 This illustration shows stitches neatly picked up around a curved edge, ready to be worked.

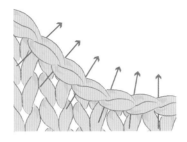

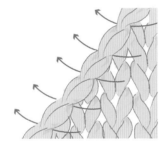

2 Insert a crochet hook or a needle just under the bound-off stitches, hiding any irregular edges.

3 This illustration shows a few of the picked-up stitches at a V-point, ready to be worked.

4 Pick up the stitches just under the bound-off stitches on a straight edge, keeping them in line.

Patterns specify the number of stitches to be picked up around the neckline after the back and front of the sweater have been sewn together. Necklines connected only at one shoulder are worked back and forth. Necklines connected at both shoulders are worked with circular needles.

The process of spacing is easier if you break it down into small sections. Work with a portion of the neckline, say the center back to the center front. Fold that half of the neckline again in half and mark the midpoint with a piece of yarn.

Then take a quarter of the neckline and fold that in two. Mark as before. Keep folding and marking shorter lengths of your portion until the spaces between the yarn markers are about 2" (5cm) in length. Repeat the folding and marking process until there are fairly even spaces between the yarn markers all around the neckline.

Example
A total of 104 stitches needs to be picked up. Divide 104 by the number of spaces between the markers. Say there are 11 spaces or

sections = 9 stitches and a remainder. Nine stitches in each of 11 spaces gives you 99 stitches, with 5 left over. Put 9 stitches in the first space, 10 stitches in the second, and continue alternating until 5 spaces each have 9 stitches and 5 spaces each have 10 stitches. Only one more space remains and the remaining 9 stitches fit into it neatly.

Picking up with stitches on holders
If your project has said to place center front and back stitches on a holder, you need to subtract these stitches from the total number of stitches needed for the neckline. The remaining stitches need to be picked up along the shaped and vertical neckline of the shoulder areas. Distribute these picked-up stitches evenly, working half on the right shoulder neckline, and half on the left shoulder. (Because the front neck opening is deeper, more stitches will be picked up on the front piece than on the back section.)

Work around the neck clockwise. Pick up the determined number of stitches for the front shoulder, working to the front holder. Place the holder stitches on the left needle without twisting them, and knit across them. Then pick up the stitches for the other front shoulder, and for the back shoulder, working to the back holder. Transfer back holder stitches to the left needle and knit across them. Pick up the remaining stitches on the second back shoulder.

CORRECTING ERRORS

I love the rhythm that builds with needles and yarn when I gather momentum on a piece of easy knitting. It happens most often when I'm having a relaxed conversation, watching the tube, or taking a long ride in the car. After a while, I sometimes feel so good I become smug about how well the knitting is going. That's usually when a mistake strikes.

The movement of the needles under my fingers has so transported me that I have forgotten to step back mentally now and then to check my work for dropped stitches and other mistakes.

When a mistake happens, allow yourself to vent, and then fix the problem and move on. There are ways to prevent or minimize mistakes, and the more tricks you add to your repertoire, the more time and work you'll save yourself.

Keep track of the pattern details; things like row counts in stitch patterns and the number of increases or decreases you have completed. Whether you use a counter, a graph, or jot down notes, this data will be welcome when you need to re-orient yourself after an interruption.

If your stitch count is off by one or two, you can compensate by increasing or decreasing without affecting the fit of the garment. Before you choose this option, however, make sure the culprit is not a dropped stitch that has left a big hole in your work.

To help prevent dropped stitches, always finish a row before you put down your knitting. If you must stop before the end of a row, put point protectors on the tips of the needles. Learn to spot any incorrectly worked stitches and fix

them. If you are a beginner, it is a good idea to work without distractions so you can give your knitting full attention until it

becomes automatic. This will allow you to spot mistakes as they occur and correct them on the spot. Good luck with the work.

CORRECTING A TWISTED KNIT STITCH

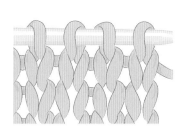

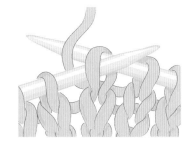

1. In a correctly-placed knit stitch, the front arm is on your right and the back arm is on your left. Above, the second stitch from the left is on the needle backward, as is the stitch on the far right.

2. To correct a twisted knit stitch, knit it through the back of the loop rather than the normal front of the stitch.

CORRECTING A TWISTED PURL STITCH

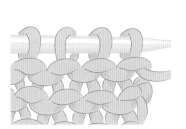

1. A purl stitch goes around the needle with the front loop on your right and the back loop on your left. Above, the second stitch from the left is twisted.

2. To untwist a purl stitch, purl it through the back of the loop. If you notice a twisted stitch worked several rows below, see the remedy in *Unraveling* on the opposite page.

PICKING UP A DROPPED KNIT STITCH

Your knitting needles can work together to pick up a stitch that has dropped one row but no further. How to pick up a dropped purl stitch is on the next page.

1. With a knit stitch that has been dropped, make sure the horizontal bar runs in the back.

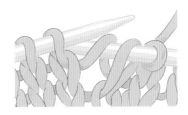

2. Put the tip of the right needle front to back through the dropped stitch and run it under the horizontal strand in the back.

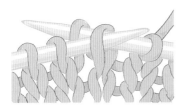

3. Put the tip of the left needle back to front through the dropped stitch. The left needle should cross the front of the right needle. With the left needle, lift the dropped stitch over the strand and off the right needle.

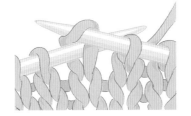

4. The new stitch is now on the right needle, but it's backward. Untwist it and move it to the left needle by inserting the left needle front to back through the center of the stitch and removing the right needle.

Unwanted extra stitches

If you get ready for a knit row by bringing the yarn over the top of the needle to the back, the edge stitch might look like two loops instead of one. It's a set-up for adding an unwanted stitch on the next row.

Always move the yarn around the side of the work, under the needle, to bring it to the back. At the start of a purl row, bringing the yarn over the top of the needle to the front will look like there are two stitches at the edge when there is really only one. An unwanted extra stitch is likely to work its way into the next row.

To prevent confusion and possible mistakes, always bring the yarn to the front by going around the side of the work, under the needle.

UNRAVELING A KNIT, AND A PURL, STITCH

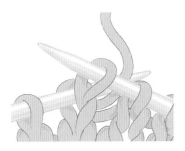

Knit stitch. With yarn at back, insert left needle into the stitch one row below the stitch on the right needle. Then drop the stitch, pulling the yarn to unravel it.

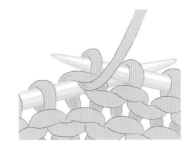

Purl stitch. With yarn in front, insert the left needle into the stitch one row below the stitch on the right needle. Then drop the stitch, pulling the yarn to unravel it.

Unraveling Stitches

A running stitch can be picked up only as long as there is slack in the horizontal strands of yarn above it. If it has fallen too far, the stitches on either side will close the gap and the dropped stitch cannot be brought up all the way.

You can either undo back to the dropped stitch or tack the loop down in the middle of the fabric, using matching yarn threaded onto

UNRAVELING ROWS

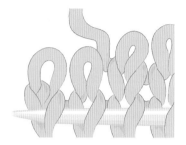

1. Insert the right needle under the first loop and over the second loop of each knit stitch in the row. Pull the working yarn and all stitches above the needle will unravel.

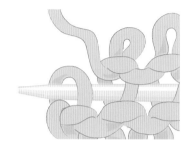

2. Use the same method for purl stitches, making sure the needle weaves through the entire row, as for the knit row.

PICKING UP A DROPPED PURL STITCH

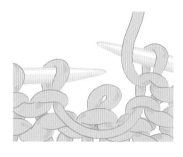

1. The needles can work together to fix a purl stitch when it has dropped only one row. With a dropped purl stitch, the horizontal bar should cross in front.

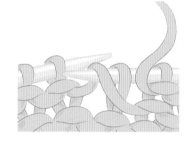

2. Insert the right needle from back to front through the dropped stitch and run it under the horizontal strand.

3. Insert the left needle (behind the right needle) front to back through the dropped stitch. Lift the stitch over the horizontal strand and off the right needle.

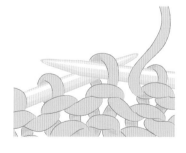

4. Slip the new stitch from the right to the left needle by inserting the left needle front to back and removing the right needle.

a tapestry needle. Simply add a stitch to your work to compensate for the dropped one.

The running-stitch pickup is useful for correcting twisted stitches and errors in stitch patterns that are several rows, or even several dozen rows, below.

Find the column of stitches that runs vertically between the mistake and your needles. Work to that spot, and drop the top stitch in the column all the way back to the error. Correct the mistake using a crochet hook and the running stitch method. If more than one stitch has a mistake, repair each one column by column. Any irregularities in the stitches that result from this fix will disappear in blocking.

Ripping out your work

Eventually, everyone has to undo work back to an error. If you're lucky you'll catch a mistake before you've finished a row and can work your way back stitch by stitch.

On a knit stitch, insert the left needle from front to back in the stitch one row below the first loop on the right needle. Remove the right needle and unravel the loop. On a purl stitch, insert the left needle from front to back in the stitch a row below the first loop on the right needle. Remove the right needle from the loop and unravel it.

If you must rip out more than one row, you don't have to put all the stitches back on the needle one by one. Select a needle smaller than the ones you've been using. Insert the tip of the needle in all the stitches across the row in which you will begin working again. In each knit stitch, make sure the tip of the needle goes through the center of the stitches without twisting them.

If you use a double-pointed or circular needle as your place-holder, you will be ready to knit whether the unraveled yarn stops on the right or left side of the work. Don't forget to use the correct size needle when you begin knitting again.

This technique can also be used with purl stitches. Insert the needle across a row directly below a line of purl bumps. Insert the needle through each purl stitch without twisting it. Work the needle across the row and rip back to the loops on the needle.

PICKING UP RUNNING STITCHES

Running stitches are stitches that have dropped more than one row. To rein them in, you need a crochet hook to serve as your "third" hand.

Repairing running knit stitches

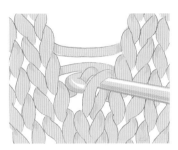

1. To repair a knit stitch that has gone running, make sure it is in front of the loose horizontal strands on the rows above.

2. Insert a crochet hook from front to back. Hook the lowest horizontal strand and pull it through the loop. Repeat until all the horizontal strands have been taken up in order, from the bottom up. Place the stitch on the left needle, making sure it is not twisted.

Repairing running purl stitches

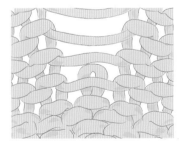

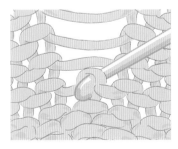

1. With a running purl stitch, make sure the loose horizontal strands fall in front.

2. Put the crochet hook through the dropped stitch from back to front. Hook the horizontal strand and pull it through the stitch. Repeat with all the horizontal strands, being careful to use them in order, from the bottom up. Place the stitch on the left needle, making sure it is not twisted.

BORDERS & EMBELLISHMENTS

Along with neat seams, attention to borders and embellishments can give a professional look even to "so-so" knitting. Taking time with these details can be rewarding and fun.

A crochet border brings uniformity to edges where the knitting can't guarantee a neat finish. Depending on the color of a border, the edges can recede or become part of the design. Usually, you work crochet borders with the right side facing. If you hold the work with the knitted stitches vertical, anchor the border in the center of the stitches on the top row, below the bind-off. If inserting the hook through the center of the knit stitches makes the border flare or ripple, put the hook through the spaces between the stitches. If the stitches run horizontally, insert the hook inside the outer edge of the stitches.

SINGLE CROCHET

Single crochet is the name for a foundation crochet stitch. One row of single crochet makes a narrow border.

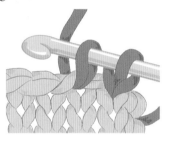 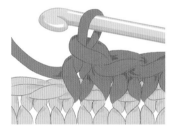

To anchor the border, insert the crochet hook from front to back in a corner stitch. Hook a loop of yarn, bringing the strand over the back of the hook to the front. Draw the loop through to the right side. With the hook free of the knitting, hook the yarn as before. Draw the new loop through the old one. The foundation for the border, right corner, has been completed with one chain stitch.

    With the chain stitch still on the hook, insert the tip of the hook again through the knitting from front to back. Hook the yarn and draw the new loop through to the front as shown above.

Hook the yarn and draw the newest loop through the other two loops. The completed single crochet is shown above. Continue to work single crochet stitches along edge in this manner.

SLIP STITCH

Slip stitch is also a basic crochet stitch. It makes a narrower border than single crochet and is particularly useful in drawing in an overlarge or drooping edge. Anchor a slip stitch border with a single chain stitch as you would for a single crochet border.

With the chain stitch on the hook, insert hook from back to front through the edge of the knitting. Hook a loop of yarn, bringing the strand over the hook from front to back. Draw up the loop near the hook and pull it through the first loop in one continuous movement. Continue to work neatly in this way along the edge.

KNITTING AN I-CORD

I-cord, a versatile edging and embellishment, is a narrow tube of circular knitting that is simple to make and is a useful item. Here's how to make one.

Using a double-pointed needle of a size similar to the one you have been using, cast on three to five stitches. Knit one row with a second double-pointed needle. * Do not turn the work. Slide the stitches from the left end to the right end of the double-pointed needle in the right hand.

With the work facing in the same direction, transfer the needle with the stitches to the left hand. The working yarn hangs on the left side. Pull it tightly to the right and knit another row.

Repeat from * for desired length. To end, cut yarn, leaving a tail. Draw the tail through all the stitches on needle to draw sts tightly together. Fasten off.

BUTTONHOLES

The first step for buttonholes is selecting the right buttons for the style of sweater or cardigan you are creating. Once you have chosen the style you like, you can decide the style of buttonhole you will make. The width of the buttonhole should allow the button to slide through the buttonhole, touching both ends, without force. Try a practice run with a buttonband swatch and the buttons chosen for the sweater.

Patterns state where to place the top and bottom holes but will ask you to "evenly space" the ones in between. Look at a finished cardigan and count the number of spaces between the top and bottom buttonholes.

Say you're working on a V-neck cardigan with a buttonhole band measuring 17" (43cm) long. The first buttonhole is 1" (2.5cm) from the bottom, and the last is ½" (1.25cm) below the V of the V-neck.

There are six buttonholes planned, four of them are to be placed between the top and bottom buttonholes.

To figure the length between the top and bottom buttonholes, subtract the small areas above and below the first and sixth holes from the length of the buttonhole band: 1½" (3.75cm). A 17" (43cm) band, less 1½" (3.75cm) = 15½" (39.5cm) long. Divide 15½" into five spaces, which is about 3" (7.75cm) between buttonholes.

Refer to the gauge to find out how many rows you get in 3" (7.75cm). Say it is 4 rows to 1" (2.25 cm). A 3" (7.75cm) space between buttonholes needs 12 rows. Thus five 3" (7.75 cm) spaces = 15 inches (38 cm), with ½" (1.25cm) left. Move the top buttonhole two rows down.

EYELET BUTTONHOLES

Eyelet buttonholes are easy to make and fine for small buttons and sweaters for young children.
Row 1: Work to the buttonhole. Knit two together, yarn over, work to end of row.

Row 2: Work to the buttonhole. Work a stitch in the yarn over and complete the row. One buttonhole is completed.

Left
A selection of buttons old and new.
Below
Smiling kitten's faces add a cute touch to a child's cardigan.

Glossary of Terms

In this list you will find most of the terms you will come across when you are reading a pattern.

A **Above markers** knitting worked after markers were placed in certain stitches

Above ribbing work done after the last row of ribbing

Along neck used in describing an unfinished neckline where stitches are picked up

Around neck used in describing a curved neckline where stitches are picked up

As established continue to work in the sequence or pattern previously described

As foll work the following instructions

As for back; as for front work piece identical to the one mentioned in the instructions

Asterisks * * commonly used in knitting instructions to designate the beginning and end of sequences that are repeated

At the same time work the instructions that follow over the same rows that apply to the instructions immediately preceding

B **Back edge** any edge on the back piece of a garment

Bind off (number of) stitches at beg of next (number of) rows used when shaping armholes and shoulders. Stitches are almost always bound off at the beginning of a row.

Both sides at once, or both sides at the same time used when stitches have been bound off in the middle of a piece for a neckline or other opening. The stitches on each side of the opening are to be worked simultaneously with separate balls of yarn.

C **Cap shaping** the shaped part of a sleeve between the underarm and the shoulder. The shaping is intended to make the sleeve fit into the armhole.

Center back neck or center front neck the point that occurs at the center back or center front of the neckline

Centimeter (cm) metric unit of measurement that often appears alongside inches in gauge schematic on yarn labels and garment schematics in patterns

D **Directions are for smallest size with larger sizes in parenthesis** in instructions given for more than one size, the smallest is listed first and the rest are grouped inside the parentheses in ascending order

Do not turn work keep the work facing in the same direction as the row just completed

E **Each side or each end** work according to the directions both at the beginning and end of a row

End with RS row or end with WS row the work is finished when you have completed a right side (RS) or wrong side (WS) row

Every other row when increasing or decreasing, leave one row between shaping rows

F **Fasten off** to secure the stitches at the end of a bind-off row when one stitch remains on the needle; cut yarn and draw end through the last stitch to tighten.

Finished bust circumference of a sweater at the bustline after it has been assembled

Front edge any edge on a front piece of a garment

Full-fashioned used when decreases are made a few stitches from the edge and are treated as a decorative element

G **Gauge** number of stitches and rows over one square inch or a larger specified area of knitting

H **Hold to back of work, hold to front of work** applies to stitches on cable needle held to front or back of work as it faces you

I **Inc . . . sts evenly across row** increase a certain number of stitches at even intervals across a row

In the same way or manner: repeat the process previously described

K **Knitwise** work as if you were making a knit stitch

K the knit sts and p the purl sts when a pattern like ribbing, (k1, p1) has been established, make the same stitch as the stitch in the row below, facing you

L **Left** the left side of the finished garment as it is worn

M **Make one:** increase one stitch by twisting the horizontal bar between existing stitches into a loop and knitting into the loop

Multiple of . . . sts the number of stitches necessary for working a pattern once, or a single pattern repeat. The total number of stitches should be divisible by the number of stitches required to work a pattern once.

Multiple of . . . sts plus . . . extra   the number of stitches required for working a pattern once and the number extra stitches to be worked only once on one or both ends to frame the pattern

P   Pattern repeat   number of stitches needed to work a pattern once

Place marker(s)   put a marker on the needle between stitches as a reminder to make an increase, a decrease, or some other change in the pattern

Preparation row   row that sets up a stitch pattern but is not part of the actual pattern

Purlwise   work as if making a purl stitch

R   Rep between *'s   Repeat all the instructions written between the two asterisks

Rep from * around   used when knitting with circular needles and means repeat the instructions after the asterisk until the end of the round, the point at which the cast-on stitches were joined

Repeat from * to end   repeat instructions from the * as many times as possible until the end of the row

Repeat from . . . row   repeat previously worked instructions from the row with the designated number

Rep inc or rep dec   repeat the increase or decrease as previously instructed

Rep . . . times more   repeat the just-worked instructions as many times as designated

Reverse shaping   used when pattern calls for two pieces that are mirror images of each other, as for right and left fronts

Right   directional term that refers to the right-hand side of a garment as you are wearing it

Right side (RS)   refers to the side of the finished garment that faces outside when it is being worn

Row 1 and all RS, or odd-numbered, rows   used when all right-side, or odd-numbered rows are worked the same way

Row 2 and all WS, or even-numbered, rows   used when all wrong-side or even-numbered rows are worked the same way

S   Same as   repeat the instructions given in another section of the pattern

Schematic   scale drawing showing measurements of all pieces of a pattern before they are assembled

Selvage st(s)   an extra stitch (or stitches) at the sides of a piece used either to make a decorative edge or to make seaming easier

Slip marker(s)   move marker from one needle to the other as you come across it to keep it in the same position one row after the other

Sew tops of sleeves between markers   used when there is no armhole shaping

Swatch   a sample of knitting used to test gauge or try out a pattern or colorwork

T   Through . . . row   work up to and including the row with the specified number

To . . . row   complete the row just before the row with the designated number and stop

Total length   length of a finished garment from top to bottom

Turn or turning   transfer or transferring your work after a row has been completed from the right hand to the left hand. The right needle with all the stitches becomes the left needle for the next row. The tip of the needle changes direction in this transfer (to face the tip of the other needle) but the working yarn remains in the center of your line of vision.

Turning ridge   row of purl stitches on the knit side of stockinette stitch along which a piece is folded for a hem

W   Weave in ends   on the wrong side, work tails into stitches so they do not unravel and do not show on the outside

When armhole measures   length of back or front of garment from beginning of armhole shaping

With right side (RS) facing   the side that will face outside when the item is done now faces you for the specified procedure. Used when picking up stitches.

With wrong side (WS) facing   the side of the work that will face inside when the garment is completed.

Work buttonholes opposite markers   buttonholes should be worked directly opposite the markers placed on a buttonband so that buttons and buttonholes will have identical spacing and line up

Work even or work straight   continue working in pattern without any increase or decrease in stitches or other shaping

Work to correspond   work one piece, or one side of a symmetrical shape, so that it fits with the other side (forms a mirror image)

Working yarn   yarn used to form new stitches; almost always the strand leading to a bobbin, ball, or skein

Wrong side (WS)   side of the finished garment that will face inside when the garment is worn

ABBREVIATIONS

[ ]	Work instructions within brackets as many times as indicated
* *	Repeat instructions between asterisks as directed
*	Repeat instructions following the single asterisk as indicated
alt	alternate, alternately
beg	begin/beginning
CC	contrasting color
cm	centimeter
cn	cable needle
CO	cast on
cont	continue(ing)
dec	decrease, decreases, decreased, decreasing
dpn	double-pointed needle(s)
foll	follow/follows/following
g	gram
inc	increase/increases/increasing
k	knit
k2tog	knit 2 stitches together
kwise	knitwise
lp(s)	loop(s)
m	meter
M1	make one stitch, an increase
MC	main color
mm	millimeter(s)
oz	ounce(s)
p	purl
pm	place marker
p2tog	purl 2 stitches together
psso	pass slip stitch over
pwise	purlwise
rem	remain, remaining, remains
rev St st	reverse stockinette stitch
rnd(s)	round(s) in circular knitting
RS	right side
sc	single crochet
sk	skip
sl1, k1, psso	slip one, knit 1, pass slip stitch over the knit stitch
sl1, k2tog, psso	slip one, knit 2 together, pass slip

	stitch over the two stitches knitted together
sl	slip one or more stitches without working them
sl1k	slip 1 knitwise
sl1p	slip 1 purlwise
sl st	slip stitch
ssk	slip next two stitches knitwise individually from left to right needle, then insert tip of left needle through fronts of loops from right to left. Knit them.
st(s)	stitch or stitches
St st	stockinette stitch or stocking stitch
tbl	through the back loop
tog	together
WS	wrong side
wyib	with yarn in back
wyif	with yarn in front
yd(s)	yard(s)
yfwd	yarn forward
yo	yarn over
yon	yarn over needle

SKILL LEVELS FOR KNITTING AS USED IN PROJECTS

Beginner ◖■□□▷
Projects for first-time knitters using basic knit and purl stitches. Minimal shaping.

Easy ◖■□▷
Projects using basic stitches, repetitive stitch patterns, simple color changes, and simple shaping and finishing.

Intermediate ◖■■▷
Projects with a variety of stitches, such as basic cables and lace, simple intarsia, double-pointed needles and knitting in the round needle techniques, mid-level shaping and finishing.

CARING FOR YOUR GARMENTS

So now you have your wonderful knitted garment. You have spent many hours and a lot of brain power working it out and knitting it—now is the time to think about looking after it. A good quality, handmade knitted garment will last for years if it is cared for in the correct way. Caring for the garment starts when you buy the yarn. Look at the label and make a note of the washing or dry cleaning instructions.

Washing

You must have accidentally washed a pure wool sweater in the washing machine by now. If you haven't—don't (unless the label specifies it is machine washable). Friction, agitation, and heat can cause it to look like a matted mess for a monster. Unless that is the required fashionable look, I would advise you wash any woolen garment by hand. Use soap flakes, mild detergent, and specially formulated liquid washing liquids that show baby soft woolens on the packet.

Use cool water and make sure the detergent or soap flakes are thoroughly dissolved before you place the garment in the water. If you find that cold water doesn't dissolve the flakes, add some hot water and stir until they are well dissolved, and let it stand until the water is cold.

To help keep a garment's shape, do not wring or rub the fabric. It is best not to soak yarn, so wash an item as quickly as possible. Rinse well and make sure the detergent or soap is completely rinsed from the garment before drying it.

Cotton and other fibers can be washed in a machine (again, check the label). Use the wool or delicate cycle (using cold water) with just a

Below
After handwashing, roll a washed garment in a dry towel to dry.

little spin action. I place woolen garments in a net washing bag with a zip.

Drying

Dry garments on a towel placed on a flat surface or on a sweater dryer, a mesh fabric stretched across a frame. This way, they keep their shape. When dry, you can steam out wrinkles with an iron just hovering above the surface. Don't let the iron touch the yarn.

Storing

It is advisable to keep garments in a clothes storage box, or wrap them in tissue and place them in a plastic

Below
Clear bags with a zipper are good to store handknitted garments.

bag that can be tucked in a drawer or placed on a shelf in a wardrobe. Be on guard against moths, which are attracted to dirt and natural oils often found in the more natural types of yarns.

Consider placing a ball of cedar wood, or a packet of moth balls, in the drawer or wardrobe where your knitted things are kept. The fragrance of these balls has improved over the decades and your clothes no longer smell like your grandmother's had them in the drawers forever. If your garments do smell slightly, hang them in fresh air for an hour or so and the odor will fade.

THE PROJECTS

Practice the basics by making a little something warm or elegant, as the mood suits you. The projects in this section include a fabulous man's sweater for cold winter days, a cute pink and white striped hat, a sleeveless shell top, a child's cardigan, a stylish topper, and a chic women's cardigan.

Materials:

Yarn:	Rowan Polar, 109yd(100m)/ 3.5oz (100g) ball
Color:	Purple 643
	White 645
Amount:	1 ball purple, 2 balls white
Total yardage:	109yd (100m) purple, 218yd (200m) white
Needles:	US 11 (8mm) needles or size to obtain gauge
Gauge:	15 stitches = 4" (10cm)
Finished size:	8" (20cm) x 54" (135cm)

Pattern stitch: Garter st: Knit every row.

Note: Each time you change colors, cut off the old color, leaving a 6" (15cm) tail.

INSTRUCTIONS

Cast on 30 stitches in Polar white.
In garter stitch (knit every row):
Work 18 rows (9 ridges) white, then add second color and work 4 rows (2 ridges) purple, 18 rows white, 4 rows purple, 18 rows white, 4 rows purple, 10 rows white, 4 rows purple, 8 rows white, 8 rows purple, 110 rows in white, 8 rows purple, 8 rows white, 4 rows purple, 10 rows white, 4 rows purple, 18 rows white, 4 rows purple, 18 rows white, 4 rows purple, 18 rows white. Bind off sts.

TIPS

Take note of the number of rows you do in each color. Overall, this will prevent the tedium of knitting the same stitch all the time. Use a row counter, too. Keep in mind that every two rows in garter stitch creates one ridge so you can count ridges.

And, if the stitch at the end of the row is a bit loose, knit the first two stitches on the next row very tightly and the loose one on the row below will pull up. The edges on this scarf are left as knitted, so it is important to maintain a firm edge.

Fringe

To make fringe at each end of the scarf, cut 32 12" (30cm) pieces of yarn in purple and 28 lengths of white. Working 8 purple and 7 white fringes at each end (see photograph for color placement), fold each length in half and use a crochet hook to draw the folded end, from right side to wrong side, through the edge of the scarf. Draw the cut ends through the loop formed by the folded end and pull to tighten the knot.

Weaving in ends

Thread yarn-end (tail) into a tapestry needle and hide the yarn by weaving it in and out along the bumps of the same-colored knit stitches.

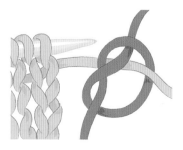

Left

Joining a new thread: Make a temporary knot at the side of work. To finish, untie knots and weave in ends.

A LONG, FRINGED SCARF

Here's a warm scarf to wrap around your neck when the cold weather starts. Knitted in chunky yarn, it feels soft and will keep out the chill.

A SHORT
SILKEN
SCARF

*The openwork in this scarf only
looks tricky. It is simple seed
stitch, alternating knit and purl
stitches, worked on large needles
with a colorful ribbon yarn.
The combination of color and
texture makes a stylish statement
for an entire ensemble.*

Below
Loose, oversized stitches make the most of this slinky ribbon yarn.

Skill level: ■□□□

Materials:

Yarn:	Berroco Zen Colors 110yd (100m)/1.75oz (50g) hank
Color:	Mt. Fuji Mix 8141
Amount:	1 hank for up to 40" (101cm) in length
Total yardage	110yd (100m)
Needle size:	US 17 (12.75mm) or size to obtain gauge
Gauge:	About 12 stitches = 4" (10cm)
Finished size:	About 5½" (14cm) wide by 40" (1m) long

YARN TIPS

Remember to bring the yarn between the two needles to the back before starting a knit stitch. Move it between the two needles to the front before starting a purl stitch. For an open-work scarf like this gauge is not critical.

Note that if the dimensions are wider or longer than the specified size, a second hank of yarn will be needed.

Managing ribbon yarn: I love working with ribbon, but I don't like its tendency to twist ever more tightly as I knit, or its habit of falling into a mass of tangles when I'm half-way through a ball. I solve both problems by putting the ribbon into a plastic bag with a zipper. The bag prevents the ball from rolling out. And in the closed position, the zipper holds the ribbon taut while I bat the ball around to untwist the working strand. The tails of ribbon yarn worked on large needles may not hold if they are woven into the fabric the usual way. If you find this to be the case, secure the tails with a sewing needle and invisible thread.

Pattern stitch

Seed stitch over odd number of stitches.
Row 1 and all subsequent rows: K1, *p1, k1, repeat from * to end.

INSTRUCTIONS

Cast on 15 stitches. Work in seed stitch for 40" (100cm) or desired length.

Bind off

Bind off in pattern stitch as follows: K first st * pass yarn between needles to front of work, p next st, lift k st over p st and drop it (1 st bound off), move yarn between needles to back of work and k next st, pass p st over k st and drop it (another st bound off), repeat from * to end.

Pattern Stitch:
Stockinette stitch: Knit one row, purl one row.

INSTRUCTIONS

Brim
With B (Gedifra Scarlet) cast on 62 (66) sts.
Row 1: Right side: Knit.
Row 2: Purl.
Repeat last two rows (stockinette stitch) until piece measures 2" (5cm).
Cut B yarn, leaving tail long enough for 2" (5cm) seam. Join A. With A, continue in stockinette st until hat measures about 7" (8") [18cm (20cm)] long, from cast-on edge, ending with a WS row.

For smaller size only:
Next row: *K3, k2 tog, repeat from * to * 11 times more, k2. 50 sts

For larger size only:
Next row: Knit.

For both sizes:
Next row: Purl.

Shape crown (both sizes):
Row 1: K 2, k2 tog, *k2 , k2tog, repeat from* until 2 sts remain, k2. 38 (50) sts
Row 2: Purl.
Row 3: K 2, k2tog,* k1, k2tog, repeat from * until 1 st remains, k1. 26 (34) sts

Skill level: ■■□□
Materials:

Yarn:	Rowan Polar, 109yd (100m)/3.5oz (100g) ball; Gedifra Scarlet 55yd (50m)/1.75oz/50g ball
Color:	Polar, Lettuce 642 (color A) Gedifra, Scarlet 1869 (color B)
Amount:	1 ball each
Total yardage:	109yd (100m) for A, 55 yards (50m) for B
Needle size:	US 11 (8mm) or size to obtain gauge
Gauge:	About 12 sts and 16 rows = 4" (10cm) in St st
Finished size:	20" (22") [51cm (56cm)] in circumference

Row 4: Purl.
Row 5: K1, *k2tog, repeat from * until 1 st remains, k1. 14 (18) sts
Row 6: Purl.
Row 7: K1, *k2tog, repeat from * until 1 st remains, k1. 8 (10) sts
Row 8: Purl.
Row 9, *K2tog, repeat from * to end. 4 (5) sts

Finishing
Leaving long tail for seam, thread tapestry needle with yarn and run it through remaining stitches. Seam with mattress stitch (see page 00).

Work the seam on the outside of the hat from the crown toward brim. Where the yarn changes color, drop A and pick up tail of B. Work remainder of seam with the wrong side facing you, so that when the brim rolls up the seam is hidden. Weave in tails of both A and B.

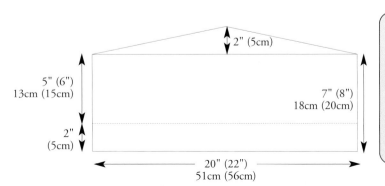

> ### TIP
>
> To keep your sewing needle on the seam lines of each side of the hat, mark them with a long running stitch in contrasting yarn. With a close-up focus, it is sometimes difficult to detect when your needle strays a bit.

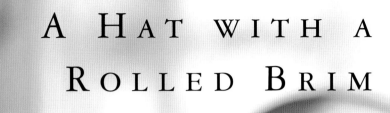

A HAT WITH A ROLLED BRIM

This version of a roll-brimmed hat covers your ears with warmth and style. It starts as a rectangle and tapers at the crown with simple decreases. An invisible seam gives this hat a professional-looking finish.

A BOATNECK SWEATER

Narrow stripes of funky yarn spell fun in this simple boatneck sweater that knits up quickly and easily in a wool-acrylic blend. The wider, ribbed neckline is an attractive design feature.

Skill level: ◖■□▷

Materials:

Yarn:	Main Color (MC): Lana Grossa Due, 60yd (55m)/1.75oz (50g) ball Contrasting color (CC): Tahki Stacy Charles Yarns Poppy 81yd (75m)/1.75oz (50g) ball
Color:	For MC color, color 37 For CC, Color 001
Amount:	12 (17, 20, 22, 27) balls MC, 1 ball CC
Total yardage:	720 (1020, 1200, 1320, 1620) yd [660 (914, 1096, 1222, 1462) m] for MC, 81yd (75m) for CC
Needles:	US 11 (8mm) needles or size to obtain gauge
Gauge:	12 stitches and 17.5 rows = 4" (10cm) in St st
Finished Size:	34" (38", 43", 47", 52") [86cm (96.5cm, 109cm, 119cm, 132cm)] at bust

Stripe pattern repeat is 14 rows long
12 rows St st in main color
2 rows rev St st in contrasting color

INSTRUCTIONS

Back

Using MC, cast on 54 (60, 66, 72, 80) sts, including one st on each end for a k st to serve as selvage or seam allowance.
Row 1: * K1, p1, repeat from * to end.
Repeat Row 1 five times more.
* Attach CC and begin stripe pattern:
Row 1: RS: With CC, purl.

Row 2: WS: Knit.
Row 3: With MC, knit.
Row 4: With MC, purl, except for first and last stitch, which are knitted for selvage.
With MC, work in St st 10 rows more.
Repeat from * for stripe pattern.
At the same time, while working with MC, wrap it underneath strand of CC at the end of each wrong-side row, bringing up strand of CC at the side of work so it will be accessible for next stripe.
Work in stripe pattern until piece measures 15" (15", 15", 16", 16") [38cm, (38cm, 38cm, 41cm, 41cm)], ending with WS.
Mark for armholes (*see tip*)
Continue working in stripe pattern until back measures 5"(5", 6", 6", 6") [13cm, (13cm, 15cm, 15cm, 15cm)] above armhole mark, ending with WS.
Next row: * K1, p1, repeat from * to end.
Repeat previous row 8 times more.
Next row: Continuing in rib pattern as established, bind off all sts.
Mark center 36 sts for neckline. There should be 9 (12, 15, 18, 22) stitches for each shoulder.

Front

Work the same as for back.

Above
This photograph shows how the boatneck fits across the front and back of the sweater.

Above
This sweater knits up in no time at all, and the ribbed edge creates an attractive hem.

TIPS

Selvage
If you knit the first and last stitches of each row you will create ridges every two rows that will help you in counting rows and in lining up the pieces correctly for seaming. (If you forget to maintain the selvage, don't fret. These edges will not show.)

More on gauge
Checking gauge doesn't end with the swatch. When you're well on your way with the first piece of the sweater, check stitch gauge (width) and row gauge (length) to make sure your knitting hasn't grown looser or tighter. Small variances can be addressed by blocking, but if your gauge wanders all over, you may need to adjust your tension or change needle sizes.

Fit
To assure a good fit, review the instructions on pages 39 and 40.

Markers
To give yourself an assist in measuring for length between underarms and neckline, put an additional marker in the center of the row identified for the bottom of the armhole. Use that marker to measure the length of the armhole.

Matching row counts for length
Once you have measured the back, if your row gauge (the number of rows per inch) remains consistent, match the length of the front by counting rows.

Blocking
Identical pieces such as sleeves or fronts, can be blocked one on top of the other with right sides together.

Sleeves: Make 2

Cast on 26 (26, 28, 30, 30) sts.

Row 1: * K1, p1, repeat from * to end.

Repeat this row 5 times more (six rows total).

Row 7: K3, inc 1, k to last 4 sts, inc. 1 in next st, k3.

Row 8: Purl, except for first and last sts, which are knitted as selvage sts.

Continue in St st and inc 1 each side of work every 4th row 0 (2, 5, 4, 4) times, then every 6th row 11 (10, 8, 9, 9) times. 50 (52, 56, 58, 58) sts. Work even until sleeve measures 16" (17", 17", 17" 17") [41cm (43, 43, 43, 43cm)]. Bind off all sts.

Finishing

Block pieces according to finished measurements selected.

Sew shoulder seams together. Sew top of sleeves to armholes, which span markers on back and front pieces, using stitches-to-rows seam (*see invisible vertical to horizontal seam, page 46*). If yarn label does not advise avoiding heat, steam seams very lightly, taking care not to touch iron to fabric.

Above
The colorful yarn makes an eye-catching design feature in the body of this sweater, which is made in a wool-acrylic blend.

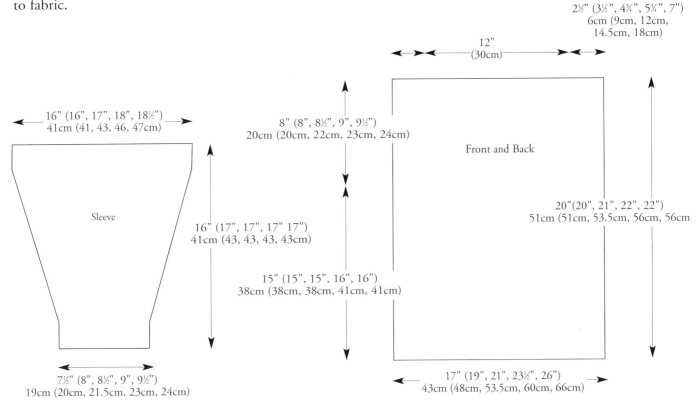

Sleeve

16" (16", 17", 18", 18½")
41cm (41, 43, 46, 47cm)

16" (17", 17", 17" 17")
41cm (43, 43, 43, 43cm)

7½" (8", 8½", 9", 9½")
19cm (20cm, 21.5cm, 23cm, 24cm)

2½" (3½", 4¾", 5¾", 7")
6cm (9cm, 12cm, 14.5cm, 18cm)

12"
(30cm)

8" (8", 8½", 9", 9½")
20cm (20cm, 22cm, 23cm, 24cm)

Front and Back

20"(20", 21", 22", 22")
51cm (51cm, 53.5cm, 56cm, 56cm

15" (15", 15", 16", 16")
38cm (38cm, 38cm, 41cm, 41cm)

17" (19", 21", 23½", 26")
43cm (48cm, 53.5cm, 60cm, 66cm)

A SLEEVELESS SUMMER TOP

This simple top skims the body, with a gently rolled neckline and garter ridges to add movement and texture to a classic shape. Wear it under a suit and go from day into evening.

INSTRUCTIONS

Back

Cast on 86 (96, 104, 114, 122) sts, including 2 stitches for selvage/ seam allowance.
Row 1: * K1, p1, repeat from * to end.
Repeat Row 1 for 1", ending with a (WS) row.
Next row: Knit.
Next row: Purl, except for first and last sts, which should be knitted for selvage/seam allowance.
Maintaining St st and selvages as established, work until piece measures 13 (14", 14", 15", 15") [33cm (35cm, 35cm, 38cm, 38 cm)], ending with WS row (*see measuring, page 74*).

Begin armhole shaping

For first three sizes: Bind off 5 (5, 6) stitches at the beginning of the next two rows. 76 (86, 92) sts.
Next row: RS: K2, pm (place marker) for selvage, k2tog, work to last 4 sts, ssk, pm, k2 for selvage. 74 (84, 90) sts remain.
Next row: WS: k2, sl marker, purl to next marker, sl marker, k 2.
Repeat previous two rows 6 (10, 10) times more. 62 (64, 70) sts remain.
For larger two sizes:
Bind off (5, 6) sts at beginning of next two rows. (104, 110) sts
Next row: Sl as if to purl, k1, pass slip stitch over (sl 1purlwise, k 1, psso), bind off 4 sts, k to end. Turn.

Skill level:	◨■▢▢
Materials:	
Yarn	Berocco Glace, 75yd (69m)/1.75oz (50g) ball
Color:	Tumeric 2591
Amount:	6 (9, 12, 13, 14) balls
Total yardage	450 (675, 900, 975, 1050) yd [411 (621, 828, 897, 966)m]
Gauge:	Measured flat: 18.5 sts and 28 rows = 4". Measured after hanging, 18.5 sts and 18.25 rows = 4"
Needles:	US 9 (5mm) or size to obtain gauge
Finished size:	Bust: 36"(40", 44", 48", 52") [91cm (102cm, 112cm, 122cm,132cm)] Length: 20" (21", 22", 23", 23") [51cm (53.5cm, 56cm, 58.5cm, 58.5cm)]

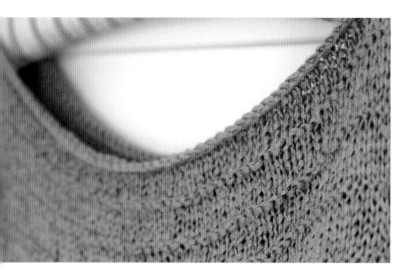

Next row: WS: Sl 1 pwise, k1, psso, bind off 4 sts in purl, p to end. (94, 100) sts

Next row: RS: K2, place marker (pm) for selvage, k2tog, k to last 4 sts, ssk, pm, k2 for selvage.

Next row: WS: K2 for selvage, sl marker, p to next marker, sl marker, k 2 for selvage.

Repeat previous two rows (9, 10) times more. (74, 78) sts.

For all sizes:

Maintaining garter stitch selvage on 2 stitches at each edge, work even (without increasing or decreasing) until piece measures 7" (7", 7", 8", 8") [18cm (18cm, 18cm, 20cm, 20cm)] from beginning of armhole shaping. When it comes time to join back and front at shoulders you can choose to seam the bound-off edges or join them as you bind off both edges.

To prepare for seaming shoulder seams:
Bind off all stitches. Mark 6 (7, 10, 12, 14) sts on each end for shoulder seams.

To prepare for three-needle bind-off: (see *Skills, opposite page*)
Work 6 (7, 10, 12, 14) sts. Bind off center 50 sts. Work remaining 6 (7, 10, 12, 14) sts. Put each set of stitches on a separate stitch holder.

Front

Work same as for back until approx. 1" (1", 2", 2", 2") [2.5cm (2.5cm, 5cm, 5cm, 5cm)] above

Left

This neckline is worked without shaping but makes a flattering dip by itself.

beginning of armhole shaping, ending with WS row.

* Next row: RS: While maintaining selvages and continuing to shape armholes as for back, purl across row.

Next row: WS: K2, sl marker, p to last 2 sts, sl marker, k2

Work 4 more rows in St st. Repeat from * until there are three more purl ridges on right side. (4 ridges total)

Work in St st until front matches length of back. Prepare for sewing shoulder seams or three-needle bind-off, as for back.

Finishing

Block pieces according to finished measurements selected. Join shoulder seams by sewing or with three needle bind-off. Sew the side seams, using mattress seam (*see page 45*).

MEASURING SYNTHETICS PRONE TO STRETCHING

I love the sheen of rayon, but you do have to take into account that is a synthetic and will stretch. Before beginning the project, make a swatch at least 6 inches by 6 inches and pin it to a pillowcase or towel draped over a hanger. Attach binder clips or other weights. Allow to hang overnight before measuring.

Use the same method, without the weights, to measure the length of the back for the armhole decreases, and again to finish the piece at the neck and shoulders. To ensure that the length of the front is identical to the back, match the number of rows below and above the start of the armhole shaping.

THREE-NEEDLE BIND-OFF

This trick is efficient and neat on shoulder seams, and wherever two pieces of knitting with equal numbers of stitches are to be joined head to head. Here's how to do it for the shoulder seams. After the pieces are blocked and ready to be assembled, put the right sides together, matching the shoulder edges Working one shoulder at a time, transfer the stitches on each side of the seam from their holder onto a knitting needle. Make sure the tips of the needles face in the same direction. Line up the needles in your left hand as if they were one. See details below.

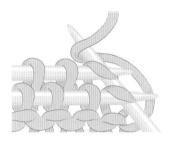 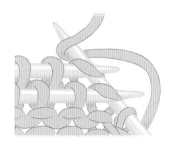 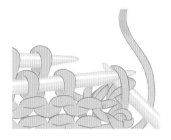

Put a third needle knitwise through the center of the first stitch on the left needle nearest you. Then insert the needle knitwise through the center of the first stitch on the needle directly behind.

Wrap the yarn to knit and pull the new loop through the old loops on both needles. Drop the old loops from the left needles. There now is one stitch on the right needle. Knit another stitch in the same way as the first.

Then lift the first stitch you made on the right needle up and over the second stitch and off the needle (1 stitch bound off).

Knit another stitch, going through the corresponding loops on both left needles, and once again lift the first stitch you made over the second one and off the needle. Continue knitting one and binding off one until there is just one loop left. Cut the yarn, leaving a tail. Draw the tail through the final loop and tighten.

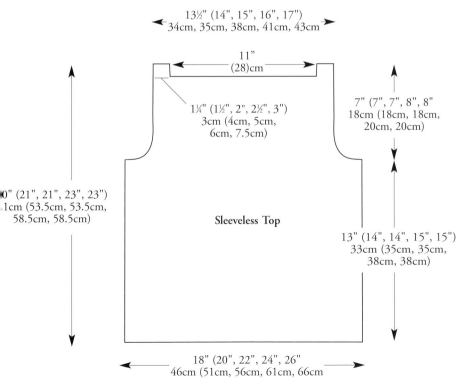

13½" (14", 15", 16", 17")
34cm, 35cm, 38cm, 41cm, 43cm

11"
(28)cm

1¼" (1½", 2", 2½", 3")
3cm (4cm, 5cm, 6cm, 7.5cm)

7" (7", 7", 8", 8")
18cm (18cm, 18cm, 20cm, 20cm)

0" (21", 21", 23", 23")
1cm (53.5cm, 53.5cm, 58.5cm, 58.5cm)

Sleeveless Top

13" (14", 14", 15", 15")
33cm (35cm, 35cm, 38cm, 38cm)

18" (20", 22", 24", 26"
46cm (51cm, 56cm, 61cm, 66cm

SELVAGES

Garter stitch selvages are used for two purposes in this garment. A one-stitch selvage doubles as a seam allowance along the sides. And two garter stitches together form decorative selvages around the armholes.

Keep warm in a luscious poncho made from Rowan's thick and soft Big Wool, a white froth striped with the palest hint of color. It is both elegant and practical, knit up thickly with alternating bands of stockinette and garter stitch.

A PERFECT PONCHO

Skill level:	■■□□
Materials:	
Yarn:	Rowan Big Wool 87yd (80m)/ 3.5oz (100g) ball
Color:	Sugar Spun 16
Amount:	8 (10, 12)balls
Total yardage:	696 (800, 1000) yd [636 (731, 914) m]
Needles:	US 15 (10mm) needles or size to obtain gauge
Gauge:	9 stitches and 16 rows = 4" (10cm)
Finished size:	Circumference at bust and including upper arms, about 46" (51", 58") [117cm (130cm, 147cm)]

INSTRUCTIONS

The poncho is made in four pieces and seamed together in mattress stitch. The polish of the final look relies on particular attention to detail in finishing. Directions for larger sizes are in parentheses.

Left Front:

Cast on 43 (51, 57) sts; this includes 41 (49, 55) pattern sts and 1 st on each end for selvage.

Row 1: K2, k2tog, k to end of row.

Row 2: P2, k until 2 sts remain, p2.

Rows 3–14: Repeat rows 1 and 2 six times more. 36 (44, 50) sts.

For small size only:

Rows 15-16: Work in St st (k1 row, p 1 row).

Row 17: RS: K2, k2tog (decrease made), k to end.

Rows 18–20: Starting with a p row, continue in St st.

Rows 21–28: Repeat rows 17 through 20 twice more. 33 sts

Rows 29–42: Repeat rows 1 through 14 once more. 26 sts

Rows 43–56: Repeat rows 15 through 28 once. 23 sts

A detail of the finished seam.

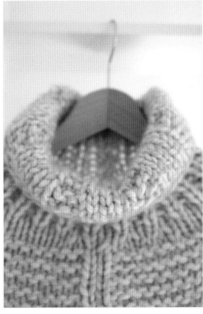

The neck rolls softly.

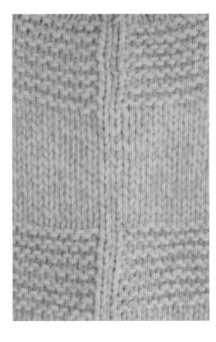

The stitch pattern up close.

For medium and large sizes only:
Row 15: K2, k2tog (decrease made), k to end.
Row 16: Purl.
Rows 17–28: Repeat rows 15 and 16 six times more. (37, 43) sts
Rows 29–42: Repeat rows 1 through 14 once. (30, 36) sts
Rows 43-56: Repeat rows 15 through 28 once. (23, 29) sts

For all sizes:
Rows 57–70: Repeat rows 1 through 14. Place remaining 16 (16, 22) sts on stitch holder. Work identical piece for right back.

Right Front
This piece has the same dimensions as the Left Front, but with reversed shaping. Work as follows:
Cast on 43 (51, 57) sts, including 41 (49, 55) pattern sts and 1 st on each end for selvage.
Row 1: K to last 4 sts, slip next 2 sts knitwise, insert needle through front of slipped sts and k them together (ssk-decrease made), k last 2 sts.
Row 2: Knit.
Now continue to work to correspond to Left Front, working same row sequence for your size, and work ssk decrease and k last 2 sts at end of decrease rows (instead of dec at the beginning). When all rows are completed, place remaining 16 (16, 22) sts on a stitch holder. Work an identical piece for the Left Back.

Finishing
Block pieces. Sew center back and center front seams using mattress stitch (see page 45).
Sew back and front together along one side, using mattress stitch.

Shape neck: Pick up all stitches on stitch holders (64, 64, 88 sts) so that you are ready to begin working with right side of poncho facing you.
Row 1: Knit, dec 11 (11, 19) sts evenly spaced.
Row 2: Purl.
Row 3: Repeat Row 1.
Row 4: Purl. 42 (42, 50) sts remain.

Turtleneck
Row 1: RS: Knit.
Row 2: WS: * P4, k2, repeat from * to end of row.
Repeat previous two rows until turtleneck measures 3" (7.5cm) long, ending with WS row.
Next row: RS: Purl.
Next row: WS: Knit.
Continue in rev St st for 4" (10cm) more. Bind off.

Sew the remaining side seam. Sew the seam in the turtleneck, reversing the right side of the seam half-way up the neck so that the wrong side is hidden when turtleneck collar is folded over.

To Make the Fringe
Cut strands of yarn 20" (51cm) long and fold in half. Insert a crochet hook at the edge of the poncho from the wrong side to the right side and draw the folded end through poncho to form a loop on the wrong side. Draw the cut ends through the loop and pull to tighten the knot.

SKILLS

If you ever feel there are too many stitches crowded on your straight needles, try knitting back and forth on a circular needle. Don't switch in the middle of your knitting, however, as a circular needle may change the gauge. To work back and forth on a circular needle, simply turn your work around at the end of each row.

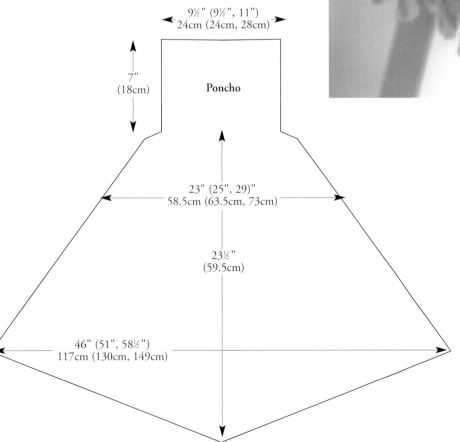

Fringe benefits

A long fringe such as this one adds a strong fashion statement to this poncho. Made of thick yarn, it swings to the motion of your body when you are walking.

9½" (9½", 11")
24cm (24cm, 28cm)

7"
(18cm)

Poncho

23" (25", 29)"
58.5cm (63.5cm, 73cm)

23½"
(59.5cm)

46" (51", 58½")
117cm (130cm, 149cm)

This updated cardigan has a rolled-in, self-finishing neckline that softens the traditional shawl collar. A single button at the bustline hardly interrupts the strong vertical line of the sweater, which is accented with wide ribs at bottom and on the sleeves.

AN ELEGANT
CASUAL CARDIGAN

Materials

Yarn:	Rowan Calmer 175yd (160m)/ 1.75 oz (50g) ball
Color:	Calm 461
Amount:	8, 9, 10 balls
Total yardage	1400, (1575, 1750) yd [1280 (1440 ,1600) m]
Other material:	1 button
Needles:	US 9 (5mm) or size to obtain gauge, and 4 stitch-holders
Gauge:	21 sts and 32 rows = 4" (10cm)
Finished size:	At bust, 38" (42", 46") [96cm (107cm, 117cm)]

INSTRUCTIONS

Back

Cast on 102 (114, 122) sts. Begin on wrong side.
Row 1: WS: K1 for selvage, p4 (0, 4), k2, * p8, k2, repeat from * to last 5 (1, 5) sts, p4 (0,4), k1.
Row 2: RS: K5, (1, 5), * p2, k8, rep from * to last 7 (3, 7) sts, p2, k5 (2, 5).
Repeat previous 2 rows for 8" (20cm), ending with WS row.
Maintaining first and last stitch of each row as a knit selvage, work in St st until piece measures 15" (38cm) from cast-on. End with a WS row.

Begin armhole shaping

Bind off 6 sts at beg of next 2 rows. Work even (without increasing or decreasing) on remaining 90 (102, 110) sts until back is 8" (9", 9") [20cm (23cm, 23cm)] longer than armhole bind-off.

Shape shoulders

(This method avoids the jog that occurs when shoulder stitches are bound off in groups.)
Row 1: Slip 1 st purlwise, k to end of row.
Row 2: Slip 1 st purlwise, p until 6 (8, 9) sts, counting sl st, remain on left needle. Turn without working these sts.
Row 3: Sl 1 st purlwise, k until 6 (8, 9) sts remain on left needle. Turn.

Row 4: Sl 1 st purlwise, p until 12 (16, 18) sts remain on left needle. Turn.
Row 5: Sl 1 st purlwise, k until 12 (16, 18) sts remain on left needle. Turn.
Row 6: Sl 1 st purlwise, purl until 18 (23, 26) sts remain on left needle. Turn.
Row 7: Sl 1 st purlwise, k until 18 (23, 26) sts remain on left needle. Turn.
Row 8: Sl 1 st purlwise, p until 24 (30, 34) sts remain on left needle. Turn.
Row 9: Sl 1 st purlwise, knit until 24 (30, 34) sts remain on left needle. Turn.
Row 10: Bind off center 42 sts. Place 24 (30, 34) sts on a holder for each shoulder.

Left Front

Cast on 58 (62, 68) sts. Beginning on WS at center front:
Row 1: WS: P 11, * k2, p8, repeat from * to last 7 (1, 7) sts, k2 (1, 2), p 4 (0, 4), k 1 (0, 1).
Row 2: RS: k5 (1, 5), p 2 (0, 2), * k8, p2, repeat from * to last 11 sts, k 11.
Repeat previous two rows until length of ribbing matches that for back, ending with a WS row.
Maintaining selvage stitch for side seam, work in St st until piece matches length of back to underarm, ending with a WS row.

Shape armhole

Bind off 6 sts at beginning of next row for armhole. Continue in St st until left front measures same length as back to shoulder shaping, ending with WS row.

Shape shoulders

Row 1: Sl 1 st purlwise, k to end of row.
Row 2: P until 6 (8, 9) sts remain on left needle. Turn without working these sts.
Row 3: Sl 1 st purlwise, k to end of row.
Row 4: P until 12 (16, 18) sts remain on left needle. Turn.
Row 5: Sl 1 st purlwise, k remaining sts.
Row 6: P until 18, (23, 26) sts remain on left needle. Turn.

Row 7: Sl 1 st purlwise, k remaining sts.

Row 8: P 28 sts. Place them on a stitch holder for collar. Place remaining 24, (30, 34) sts on separate holder for shoulder seam.

Right Front

Work as for left front, reversing shaping (*next column*). At the same time, work buttonhole on RS row immediately preceding the bind-off for armholes.

Row 1: (beginning at center front) K4, k2tog, yo twice (*see Honing skills, page 89*), k2 tog (buttonhole made), k to end of row.

Next row: K1 for selvage, purl to the two yarn-overs. P in first yo, p tbl in the second yo, p to end of row.

Sleeves: Make 2.

Cast on 52 sts.

Row 1: WS: K1, p4, * k2, p8, repeat from * until 5 sts remain, p4, k1.

Row 2: RS: K5, * p2, k8, repeat from * until 5 sts remain, k5.

Work even for 2 in (5cm), ending with WS row.

Begin sleeve increases

K selvage st and two more sts (3 sts), inc 1, work in rib pattern, as established, until 4 sts remain, inc 1 in next st, k3. 54 sts

(Note: If you choose to increase in the bar between two sts (M1), work rib pattern until 3 sts remain, then M1, and k3.)

Inc 1 st each side of sleeve every 4th row 0 (6, 12) times, then every 6th row 17 (11, 8) times, then every 8th row 2 (4, 4) times. 92 (96, 102) sts.

At the same time, end rib pattern when sleeve measures 6" (15cm) long, ending with WS row. Work in St st, maintaining selvage, until sleeve measures 18" (18", 19") [46cm (46cm, 48cm)], ending with a WS row. Bind off all stitches.

Finishing

Block pieces. Join shoulder seams using the three-needle bind-off.

Work collar: Place stitches for one side of neck onto needles and work in St st until collar is long enough to reach center back. Work other side to same length. Join two sides with three-needle bind-off or grafting (*see opposite.*) Sew sleeves to back and front between armhole bind-offs. Top of stitches on sleeves should line up against rows (sides of stitches) on back and front. Shoulder seam should hit middle of sleeve width. Indentation from armhole bind-off on back and front should fit along side of sleeves, with tops of stitches on bound-off edge lining up with sides of rows on sleeve. Sew sleeve seams to underarm. Sew side seams. Sew on button.

REVERSE SHAPING

Use the piece you have just completed as a guide to reversing the shaping. Note that the armhole shaping is worked at the start of RS rows (along the right edge as the pieces face you); to reverse the armhole shaping for the right front, work the shaping at the opposite (left) edge.

Decreases can be worked at the end of RS rows; bound-off stitches are worked at this same edge, but at the start of the following WS row. The two corresponding pieces form mirror images.

On the right front, reverse the position on the rib pattern as well by working the stitches in reverse order from those of the left front: Row 1, right front: Beginning on the WS at arm edge: Row 1: WS: K1 (0, 1), p4 (0, 4), k2 (1,2), * p8, k2, repeat from * to last 11 sts, p11. This establishes the position on the rib pattern for the right front.

The shoulder-shaping is worked to correspond to the left-front shoulder, but to place the shaping at the arm edge, start the right-front shaping on a WS row (not a RS as on the left front). What was a knit row on the left front is worked on a purl row for the right front. Work as follows: Row 1: WS: Sl 1 st purlwise, p to end of row.

Row 2: Sl 1, k until 6 (8, 9) sts remain on left needle. Turn without working these sts. Continue in this manner, working to correspond to left front, reversing knit and purl rows.

GRAFTING

For an invisible seam at the back of the neck, graft one piece to the other. The stitch illustrated below, commonly known as Kitchener stitch, reproduces the look of knitted stitches. Keep the pieces to be grafted on separate knitting needles, with points facing right. Work with the loops head-to-head on a flat surface and slip off a few stitches at a time and keep the remainder on knitting needles with point protectors. Thread a tapestry needle with matching yarn and begin working from right to left, as shown in the illustrations below.

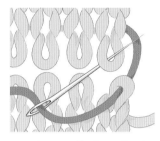

1. Insert the needle from back to front in the bottom piece. Pull the yarn through and then insert the needle from back to front in the matching stitch of the opposite piece. Pull the yarn through.

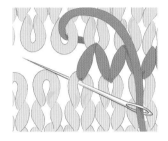

2. Put the needle from front to back through the first loop on the bottom that has been partially worked. Pull the yarn through.

3. Move the needle one stitch to the left on the bottom, and put it back to front through the center of the second stitch. Pull the yarn through.

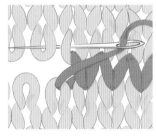

4. Put the needle front to back through center of the first partially worked stitch. Move the needle one stitch to the left on the top and insert it back to front through center of loop. Draw yarn through. Repeat steps 2 to 4 as many times as needed.

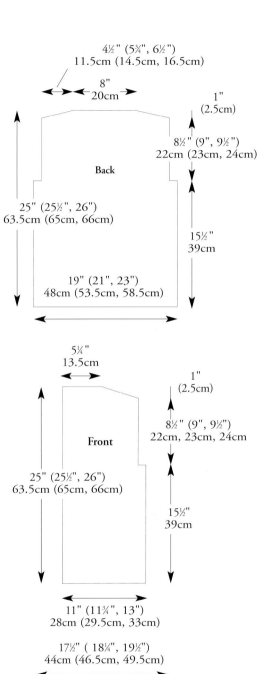

4½" (5¾", 6½")
11.5cm (14.5cm, 16.5cm)

8"
20cm

1"
(2.5cm)

Back

8½" (9", 9½")
22cm (23cm, 24cm)

25" (25½", 26")
63.5cm (65cm, 66cm)

15½"
39cm

19" (21", 23")
48cm (53.5cm, 58.5cm)

5¼"
13.5cm

1"
(2.5cm)

Front

8½" (9", 9½")
22cm, 23cm, 24cm

25" (25½", 26")
63.5cm (65cm, 66cm)

15½"
39cm

11" (11¾", 13")
28cm (29.5cm, 33cm)

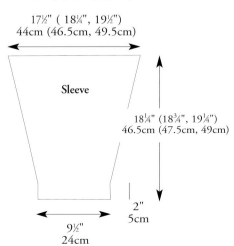

17½" (18¼", 19½")
44cm (46.5cm, 49.5cm)

Sleeve

18¼" (18¾", 19¼")
46.5cm (47.5cm, 49cm)

2"
5cm

9½"
24cm

A SOPHISTICATED EVENING BAG

The design of this small evening bag is simplicity itself and it will make a fashion statement hanging from your shoulder, especially with the right button to set off the gold of the metallic yarn. Our little envelope bag can go anywhere after dark.

Skill level: ◼◼◼◻

Materials:

Yarn: Rowan Lurex Shimmer, 104 yd (95m)/1oz (25g) ball

Color: Antique White Gold 332

Amount: 3 balls

Total yardage 312yd (285m)

Needle size: US 4 (3.5mm) needles or size to obtain gauge; same size double-pointed (dp) needles for strap

Other materials: Aluminum crochet hook size E or 4

1 button

Fabric for lining, ¼ yd (¼m), or strip of fabric at least 9" (23cm) wide

Gauge: 26 stitches and 36 rows = 4" (10cm) with two strands of yarn held together

Finished size: About 7" (18cm) wide and 4½" (11.5cm) high

Note: This envelope bag is knitted in one piece, beginning with the front and ending with the shaped flap.

Front of bag

Begin at front edge:

With 2 strands of yarn held together and size 4 needles, cast on 46 sts. Make garter stitch border:

Row 1: RS: Knit.

Row 2: WS: With yarn in front (wyif), sl 1 st purlwise, pass yarn to back between first and second sts, k to end.

Row 3: RS: Repeat previous row.

Row 4: WS: Wyif, sl 1 purlwise, pass yarn to back between first and second sts, k1: place marker (pm), p until 2sts remain on left needle, pm, k2. Turn.

Row 5: RS: Sl first st purlwise in method established, k1, sl marker (sl m), k to next marker, sl m, k2.

Maintaining slipped stitch selvage and garter stitch border, work in stockinette stitch, repeating rows 4 and 5, until piece measures 4½" (11.5cm).

Make bottom ridges:

Next row: WS: Sl first st as established, k across.

Next row: RS: Sl first st as established, k across.

Repeat last two rows once more.

Back of bag

Continue in stockinette stitch, with selvages as established, until back is as high as front, ending with WS row.

Begin flap shaping:

Row 1: Sl one purlwise, ssk (*see page 35*), work until 3 sts remain on left needle, k2tog, k1. Turn.

Row 2: Sl 1 purlwise, k1, p until 2 sts remain on left needle, k2. Turn.

Repeat previous two rows, maintaining selvages as established, until 4 sts remain. Bind off 3 sts, leaving 1 loop.

Button loop:

Insert crochet hook size 4 (E) through loop and crochet chain long enough to go around button (*see next page*). Cut yarn and pull tail through last loop to tighten. Secure to end of flap opposite the beginning of the chain.

Make I-cord shoulder strap

Using 2 double-pointed needles (dpn) in size 4 or size used to get gauge, cast on 4 sts.

Row 1: K4. * Do not turn work. Slide stitches on right needle to opposite end of dpn and put this needle in left hand.

Choose the button for this gold
evening bag carefully. The closing
button must be durable and also
chic to match the style of the bag.

Row 2: Tug working yarn firmly and k 4 sts on
left hand needle. Repeat from * until I-cord
measures 38" or desired length. (It will stretch.)
Bind off the 4 sts.

Finishing
Block the bag. Use the body of the knitted bag,
excluding flap, as a template for lining. Add a
seam allowance of about ½" (1cm) on all sides.
Cut out lining and set aside.

   With right sides out, fold the knitted bag
along the bottom ridge. Sew the side seams using
backstitch, working one stitch in from the edge
stitches.

   Knot the ends of the I-cord, allowing the
knots to extend below the bottom of the bag (still
inside out) and neatly sew the ends of the I-cord
along the side seams of bag as follows:

   Working side to side, * run a tapestry needle
threaded with one strand of yarn behind the
outermost loops on each edge stitch in the side
seams. Draw the needle and yarn through to the
other side. Working from the second side, insert
the needle behind both arms of a loop belonging
to one of the four stitches in the I-cord. Pull the
needle and yarn back to the first side. Repeat
from * as many times as necessary to attach the
I-cord along the height of the bag.

Repeat with other end of cord on other side seam.
Sew button to front of bag at spot where button
loop falls when flap is folded in place.

   To line the bag, fold the lining in half and sew
side seams, leaving ⅝"(1.5cm) at top free. Fold
down ⅝"(1.5cm) of lining at open end so that the
raw edges will face the inside of the bag.

   Insert the lining into the bag and pin the top
into place. Using a sewing needle and thread,
neatly sew the top folded edge of the lining to the
inside of the bag.

Chain Stitch
Make a slip knot and put it on a crochet hook. * Wrap
yarn from the back to front on the hook and draw the
loop through. Repeat from * for required length.

TWO-STRAND TIP

To minimize tangles when you're using two strands of yarn, put each of the two balls in its own zippered plastic bag. The bags should be large enough to allow the balls to roll around easily when you pull on the yarn, but not so large that they can fall apart easily. Finally, put the bags in a larger plastic bag. Allow enough of an opening in the larger bag so that you can pull on the two strands of yarn easily.

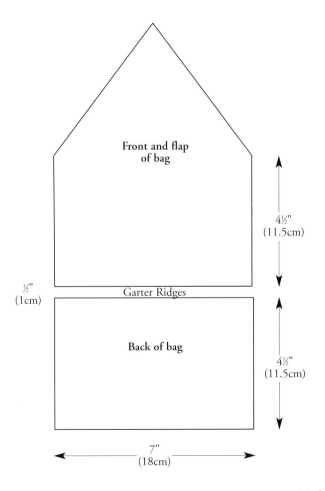

Front and flap
of bag

Garter Ridges

Back of bag

4½"
(11.5cm)

4½"
(11.5cm)

½"
(1cm)

7"
(18cm)

Right
The cord that goes over the
shoulder is cleverly attached to the
sides of the evening bag.

AN OPENWORK SCARF

Subtle changes in tone in a mohair yarn worked together with a flag novelty plays on color and texture for an effect sure to turn heads. Made long and narrow, this scarf works well folded in half around the neck, with one end tucked through the other.

Skill level:	■■□□
Materials:	
Yarn:	**A:** Reynolds Fusion 136yd/ 124m/1.75 oz (50g) ball
	A: Tahki-Stacy Charles Rialto 65yd (60m)/1.75oz (50g) ball
Color:	A: No. 5 B: No. 6
Amount:	A: 2 balls B: 3 balls
Total yardage	About 200yd (182m) of each A and B
Gauge:	About 10 sts and 11 rows = 4" (10cm)
Needle size:	US 13 (9mm) or size to obtain gauge
Finished size:	About 6" (15cm) wide and 82" (200cm) long

INSTRUCTIONS

Working with one strand each of mohair and novelty yarn held together, CO 15 sts.

Rows 1–5: Knit.

Row 6: * K1, yo (yarn over) twice, repeat from * until 1 st remains. K.

Row 7: Knit, dropping all yarn-overs.

Rows 8, 9, 10, 11: knit.

Repeat rows 6 to 11 for about 80" (200cm) or desired length. Bind off stitches. Do not block.

Honing skills

Let's look at the way yarn-overs are used in this pattern. There are two defining rows in the pattern stitch. The first one occurs when two yarn-overs follow every knit stitch. To make the double yo, bring the working yarn from back to front between the two needles, put it over the top of the right needle to the back, and repeat one more time so that there are two extra loops on the right needle after the knit stitch is made.

On the return, after the first knit stitch, you will face the two extra loops before you can get to the second knit stitch and each succeeding stitch.

Take the two extra loops off the tip of the left needle so you can get at the next stitch. At the end of the row, pull gently on the fabric with one hand and the needle with the other hand to stretch out the dropped loops.

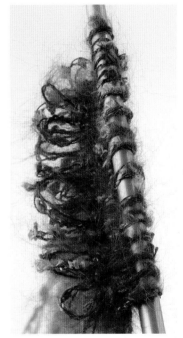

Right
The knitted stitches before you pull the yarn gently down to make the open-weave effect.

Below
The final effect in the body of the scarf.

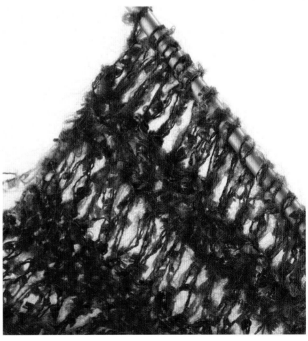

A CUTE TOPPER

This project introduces knitting in the round from the bottom up, and features a turtleneck that frames the face. Made with a wonderfully soft yarn that releases puffs of color and lends great texture to the design.

Skill level:	■■■▢
Materials:	
Yarn:	Berroco Softy 104yd (95m)/ 1.75oz (50g) ball
Color:	Love Potion 2939
Amount:	8 (10, 11) balls
Total yardage	About 832yd (1040yd, 1144yd) [(760m, 950m, 1045m)]
Gauge:	15 sts and 18 rounds = 4"
Needles	29" and 16" (73cm and 40cm) circular; US 11 (8mm) needles or size to obtain gauge
Finished size:	About 53" (59", 63") [(134.5cm, 150cm, 160cm)] at bust

Pattern stitches:

Garter st: Round 1: Knit
Round 2: Purl
Repeat these two rounds for pattern.
Reverse stockinette st (worked inside out as described below).
Knit all rounds.

Technique:

The capelet is shown in reverse stockinette stitch, with the purl side right side out. To avoid having to purl each round, knit the piece inside out, with the knit side facing you, and turn it when the work is complete. Join new balls of yarn on the side facing you.

Knitting in the round:

There are advantages to using a circular needle, one of which is that it eliminates seaming. When you have cast onto a circular needle, take care not to twist the stitches when you join them into a round. Cast on the stitches and arrange them evenly along the circular needle, with the working yarn at the needle tip on the right. Don't cast on too tightly, the stitches must slide easily from the cable to the thicker shaft. Line the stitches up facing the same way, with the bottom knots on the inside of the circle.

To help keep your place in the knitting, add a marker between the end of one round and the beginning of the next. Choose different colors to signal different purposes, one color to mark the beginning of rounds, and another color to alert you to decreases (*see illustration over page*).

INSTRUCTIONS

Using longer circular needle, cast on 273 (297, 313) sts, putting marker on needle just before last stitch is cast on. Join, knitting last cast-on stitch and first cast-on stitch together. 272 (296, 312) sts remain.

Round begins on back, left side.

Work four rounds in garter stitch, beginning with knit round. Switch to reverse stockinette stitch, worked inside out: Knit next 4 rounds.

First decrease round: * knit 36 (42, 46), k2 tog, place marker (pm), ssk (*see pages 34-35*) or other left-slanting decrease, k96 (102, 106), k2tog, pm, ssk or other left-slanting decrease, repeat from * to end. 264 (288, 304) sts

Knit 5 rounds even.

* Repeat first decrease round, dec 1 st before and after each marker as established. 8 sts decreased. Knit an additional 5 rounds.

Repeat from * 11 times more. 168 (192, 208) sts

All sizes: Next round: * Dec 1 st before and after each marker as established. 160 (184, 200) sts

Small size: K 3 rows even. * Repeat from * to * three times more. 136 sts

Medium and large sizes: * K 1 round even. Decrease 1 st before and after each marker as established. Repeat from * 4 (5) times more. 144 (152) sts

Shape for neck

Round 1: * K2, k2tog, repeat from * to end of round, ending with K2. 102 (108, 114) sts
Switch to shorter circular needle when necessary.
Round 2: K.
Round 3: * K1, k2tog, repeat from * to end of round, ending with k3. 68 (72, 76) sts
Round 4: K.

Turtleneck:

Next round: * K1, p1, repeat from * to end.
Continue in k1, p1 rib for 3¼" (8.5cm).
Next round: Purl. When piece is turned right-side out, the next section will be stockinette stitch.

Purl for 3½" (9cm) more.
Next round: K.
Next round: P.
Next round: K.
Next round: P
Next round: Bind off in knit stitch.
Turn topper inside out.

Twisted Stitches

If the cast-on stitches are twisted—a sure sign is knotted bottoms that travel around the shaft of the needle and cannot all b emade to face down—the fabric will be twisted. There's no way to fix this except ripping everything out and starting over.

JOINING

To get a join without a gap at the bottom, it is necessary to cast on one extra stitch. At the join, slip the first stitch on the right needle over to the left needle and knit them both together as illustrated below.

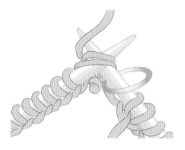

1 Cast on stitches on a circular needle, then slip marker onto the right tip. Cast on one extra stitch. Knit this together with the first stitch on left tip.

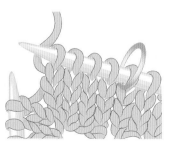

2 The marker also makes it easy to determine where one round begins and ends.

Right
Here you can
get the feeling
of the lush
raspberry color
and the softness
of the yarn,
which is perfect
for a topper to
wear on a chilly
winter's day.

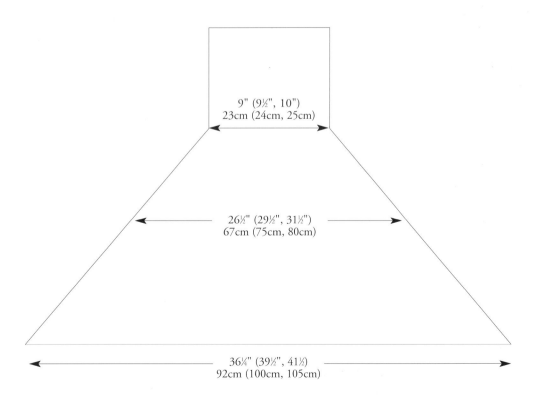

9" (9½", 10")
23cm (24cm, 25cm)

26½" (29½", 31½")
67cm (75cm, 80cm)

36¼" (39½", 41½)
92cm (100cm, 105cm)

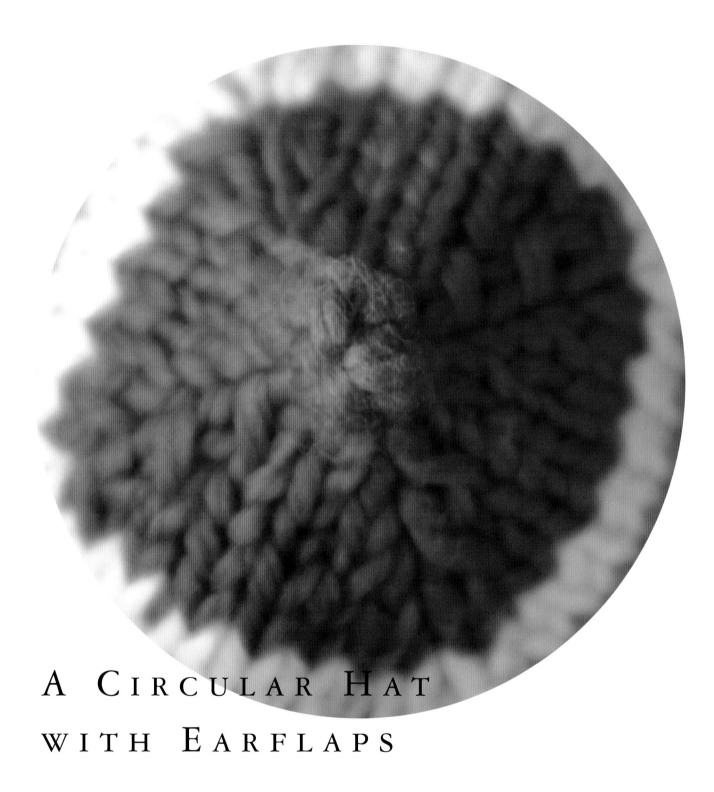

A CIRCULAR HAT
WITH EARFLAPS

Funky fun. That's what this hat is all about. The warm earflaps are knitted

separately and then put on a circular needle with cast-on stitches for the

brim. From there the hat is knit in the round, narrowing to an I-cord

nubbin at the top.

Skill level: ◖■■■▢

Materials:

Yarn:	Rowan Big Wool 87 yd (80m)/ 3.5oz (100g) ball
Color:	For A, Smooch 031
	For B, White Hot 001
	For C, Whoosh 014
Amount:	1 ball of each
Total yardage:	About 88yd (80m) of each color
Needles:	US 15 (10mm) or size to obtain gauge. One 16" (40cm) long circular needle and one set double-pointed needles (dpn)
Gauge:	About 9 stitches and 16 rounds = 4" (10cm).
Finished size:	Circumference about 19½"(21¼", 23") [49.5cm (54cm, 58.5cm)]

Pattern stitch:
Stockinette stitch (k1 row, p1 row)

INSTRUCTIONS

Earflap:
Make 2.
With A, CO 4 sts.
Row 1: K.
Row 2: P.
Row 3: K 1, make right-slanting increase in next st, (*see Lifted Increases, page 34*), k until 2 sts remain on left needle, make left-slanting inc in next st, k1. 6 sts
Row 4: P.
Row 5: K, making inc as in row 3. 8 sts
Row 6: P.
Row 7: K, making inc as in row 3. 10 sts
Row 8: P.
Row 9: K, making inc as in row 3. 12 sts Knit even (without inc or dec) until flap measures about 4" (10cm) from bottom. Leaving tail of

several inches, cut yarn and put stitches on stitch holder. Make second earflap same as the first one.

Hat
Using circular needle and A, cast on 7 (7, 9) sts for back of hat. Transfer sts for one earflap to dpn with right side facing you. Hold dpn in left hand and circular needle with cast-on sts in right hand. With working yarn from cast-on sts, work across earflap as follows: K in row below first st of earflap, k across to last earflap st, k last st in row below. Turn work so that earflap is in left hand, with WS facing you.
Cast on 17 (21, 23) sts. Turn work again so that cast-on sts and earflap are in right-hand needle.

Above
The earflaps are worked separately and joined to the hat when the stitches are cast-on for the crown.

Left

This is a hat for the young-at-heart.
Its multi-colored stripes and raised
tip will make a fashion statement
on the slopes and on the street.

Put second flap on a dpn and hold it in left hand.
Using working strand from cast-on sts, knit across
these earflap sts as for first earflap.

Join:

Transfer stitch just knitted (last earflap st) to left
needle, place marker (pm) on right needle, k
earflap st and first cast-on st tog.
Round 1: K 7, k tog next cast-on stitch with first
st of earflap, knit across earflap to last st, k tog
last earflap st with first cast-on st of front, k
across front, k tog last cast-on st of front with
first st of second earflap, k to end of round.
44, (48, 52) sts

Stripes:

Round 1: With B, k.
Round 2: K into center of first st one row below
to avoid jog in stripe (*see Skills, opposite page*).
Drop B, pick up C. With each new color, in the
first st of the second round, k in the row below,
to avoid jog in stripes.
K 6 rounds C, then
2 rounds B,
6 rounds C,
2 rounds B.
For remaining rounds, work with A only

Shape crown

When hat measures about 4" (4½", 4½") [10cm
(11.5cm, 11.5cm)] from brim, begin decreases.
Circumference will narrow until you must switch
to double-pointed needles (dpn) to handle
stitches comfortably (*see Skills*).
First dec round:
* K 7 (8, 9) sts, ssk (see page 35), place marker
(pm), make right-slanting decrease (k2tog), repeat
from * three more times. 36 (40, 44) sts

Next round: K.
Second dec round: K until 2 sts before marker, ssk (*see page 35*), slip marker (sl m), k2tog, repeat from * three more times. 28 (32, 36) sts
Next round: K.
Repeat last two rounds until 2 sts remain. Draw yarn through loops and weave in end on inside.

Finishing

With B and crochet hook, work one row of slip stitch (*see page 54*) around earflaps and bottom of the brim.

DOUBLE-POINTED NEEDLE SKILLS

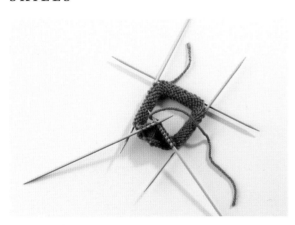

When hat narrows to about 16" (41cm) in circumference, change to a set of double-pointed needles (dpn) as follows: Knit about a third of the sts from the circular needle onto a dpn, then knit the next third onto a second dpn, and the remaining third onto a third dpn. (The round of hat sts on three dpn will form a triangle rather than a square.) With the fourth dpn (as the right-hand needle), continue to work until the first dpn (left-handed needle) is emptied and all sts are transferred to the fourth needle.

Now use the emptied needle as the right-hand needle and continue to work the sts on the next dpn and so on around, emptying each needle and using it to work the following needle. As on the circular needles, mark the beginning of rounds and avoid the jogs as you change colors.

Honing skills: Avoiding the Jog

When you start a new color at the beginning of a round, you will end up with a jog at the join with the old color unless you intervene. Knit one complete round in the new color. In the first stitch in the second round, insert the working needle one row below, into the center of the stitch of the old color. Knit the two stitches of different colors as if they were one. Inserting the needle in the row below raises the old color enough to eliminate the visual jog that otherwise would distract the eye.

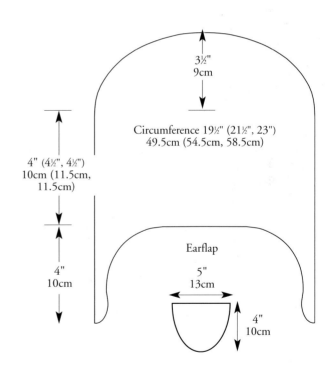

3½"
9cm

Circumference 19½" (21½", 23")
49.5cm (54.5cm, 58.5cm)

4" (4½", 4½")
10cm (11.5cm, 11.5cm)

4"
10cm

Earflap

5"
13cm

4"
10cm

CABLE CLASS

When you pick up those fabulous-looking men's sweaters,

chunky with cable stitches, and you are in awe of the work,

don't be discouraged. After this chapter you, too, will have

the opportunity to make such beautiful things.

—————

MAKING CABLES

The cable requires a little more action than many other pattern stitches, but once you learn to order those stitches around, you'll be hooked. Whether you're making a cable involving ten stitches or just crossing two of them, the principle is the same.

Ever since I learnt how to make cables as a child, I've been mesmerized by their sculptural quality. Cables are the mainstay of the richly textured fisherman's sweater, a classic style that emerged on the Aran Islands in the early 20th century. The essential technique—crossing one or more stitches over others—lends itself to infinite variation. And a bonus for relatively new knitters is that the texture of cables tends to mask uneven tension that might otherwise be all too obvious in large areas of stockinette stitch. When a cable is made, a few stitches step out of line and let a few others go ahead before they get back in the queue. The rest is just straightforward knitting and purling.

In the sweater on the next few pages, the cable is 10 stitches wide, divisible into two ropes of five stitches each, with a garter rib in the middle of each rope. For a cable, it's on the wide side, but

Left
The cable pattern in this man's sweater is impressive, especially in this type of yarn.

FOR A LEFT-SLANTING, OR FRONT, CABLE

1. Place the first half of the stitches in the cable pattern on a cable needle and leave it at the front of the work.

2. Work the remaining stitches of the pattern tugging the working yarn to close the gap left by the stitches on the cable needle.

3. With the cable needle in the left hand, knit each stitch in the same order (right to left) that it went onto the cable needle.

A RIGHT-SLANTING, OR BACK, CABLE

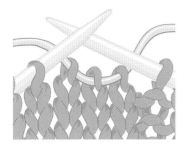

1. Put the first half of the cable on a cable needle and hold in back of the work, making sure stitches are not twisted. Work second half of cable, pulling it to the right.

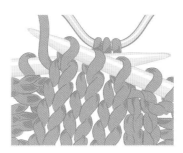

2. Push the cable needle to the back.

3. Knit each stitch in the same order (right to left) that it went onto the cable needle.

this is a man's sweater and it called for something big and bold.

There are two ways to cross a cable. There is a left-slanting, or front, cable, so-named because the stitches that step out of line wait in front of the work (*see opposite page*). In a right-slanting, or back, cable cross (*see above*), the stitches that step out of line wait to the rear of the work. In both left-slanting and right-slanting cables, the stitches are crossed on right-side rows.

If knitting stitches from a short cable needle proves difficult, use a short circular needle. The stitches on hold can stay out of the way in the middle of the circular needle without falling off.

Sometimes, with a large number of loops on hold, a circular needle can give more leverage than a cable needle in tugging the crossing stitches into place. An alternative is to switch the order of the stitches before knitting them.

After placing the first half of the stitches on a cable needle, slip the other half purlwise from the left to the right needles. Then put the stitches from the cable needle onto the left needle in backward order, so that the stitch that would have been knit first goes on the left needle last.

Finally, slip the other half of the stitches back onto the left needle. Knit across the entire cable without worrying about the cable needle.

A Man's Sweater

A ribbed cable and seed-stitch panels add vertical interest to this basic man's turtleneck pullover. The texture of the stitches makes the most of a substantial tweed yarn. Several well-placed markers will help you keep track of the pattern.

Skill level: ◼◼◼◻

Materials:

Yarn: Rowan Yorkshire Tweed Chunky, 109 yd (100m)/3.5oz (100 g) ball

Color: 550 Damp

Amount: 9 (12, 15) balls

Total yardage: About 980yd (1308, 1635) yd [895, 1195, 1494)]

Needle size: US 11 (8mm) needles or size to obtain gauge
US 9 (5mm) or two sizes smaller than larger needles
One 16" circular in each size

Gauge: 12 stitches and 16 rows = 4" (10cm) over stockinette st and seed st. 10 sts = 2" (5 cm) over width of cable

Finished size: Chest 44" (48", 53") [112cm (122cm, 134.5cm)]
Length 26½" (28", 28½") [67cm (71cm, 72cm)]
Width at upper arm: 21" (23", 23") [53.5cm (57.5cm, 58.5cm)]

Pattern stitches:

Stockinette stitch:

Row 1: RS: Knit.

Row 2: Purl.

Repeat these two rows for pattern.

Seed stitch:

All rows: K1, * p1, k1 repeat from *.

Cable:

Row 1: RS: K10.

Row 2: WS: P2, k1, p4, k1, p2.

Row 3–6: Repeat row 1 and row 2 twice more.

Row 7: Slip first 5 sts onto cable needle and hold in front, k next 5sts, k5 from cable needle.

Row 8: Repeat row 2.

Row 9–12: Repeat row 1 and row 2 twice more.

Repeat these 12 rows for pattern.

Back

Using smaller needles, cast on 67 (73, 81)stitches.

Row 1: K1, * p1, k1, repeat from * to end.

Row 2: P1, * K1, p1, repeat from * to end.

Repeat rows 1 and 2 until piece measures 2½" (6cm) from beginning.

On last row, increase 5 sts evenly spaced (*see Tips, page 105*) 72 (78, 86) sts

Change to larger needles.

Row 1: RS: Establish pattern sequence:
(Stockinette st) k10 (13, 17) sts, place marker (pm),
(seed stitch) k1, p1, k1, pm,
(stockinette st)k8, pm,
(seed st) k1,p1, k1, pm,
(stockinette st) k4, pm,
(seed st) k1, p1, k1, pm,
(cable) k2, pm, k1, pm, k4, pm, k1, pm, k2, pm,
(seed st) k1, p1, k1, pm,
(stockinette st) k4, pm,

GAUGE TIP

Make sure you note the degree to which the cable draws in the fabric when you are figuring gauge. It is best to make a sample about 8" (20cm) wide, which features all three stitch patterns.

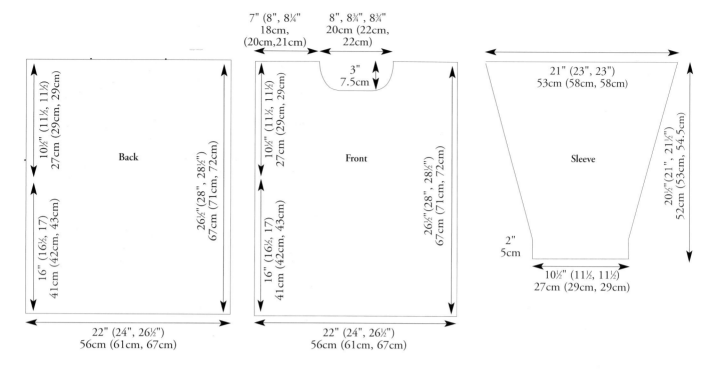

7" (8", 8¼")
18cm,
(20cm,21cm)

8", 8¾", 8¾"
20cm (22cm,
22cm)

3"
7.5cm

21" (23", 23")
53cm (58cm, 58cm)

10½" (11½, 11½)
27cm (29cm, 29cm)

Back

Front

Sleeve

10½" (11½, 11½)
27cm (29cm, 29cm)

10½" (11½, 11½)
27cm (29cm, 29cm)

26½" (28", 28½")
67cm (71cm, 72cm)

26½" (28", 28½")
67cm (71cm, 72cm)

20½"(21", 21½")
52cm (53cm, 54.5cm)

2"
5cm

16" (16½, 17)
41cm (42cm, 43cm)

16" (16½, 17)
41cm (42cm, 43cm)

22" (24", 26½")
56cm (61cm, 67cm)

22" (24", 26½")
56cm (61cm, 67cm)

(seed st) k1, p1, k1, pm,
(stockinette st) k8, pm,
(seed st) k1, p1, k1, pm,
(stockinette st) k10, (13, 17).

Row 2: WS:
(St st) p 10 (13, 17), slip marker (sl m),
(seed) k1, p1, k1, sl m,
(St st) p8, sl m,
(seed) k1, p1, k1, sl m, (St st) p 4, sl m,
(seed) k1, p1, k1, sl m,
(cable) p2, sl m, k1, sl m, p4, sl m, k1, sl m, p2,
(seed) sl m, k1, p1, k1, sl m,
(St st) p 4, sl m,
(seed) k1, p1, k1, sl m,
(St st) p 8, sl m,
(seed) k1, p1, k1, sl m,
(St st) p10 (13, 17).
Work in pattern stitches as established until piece measures 16" (16½", 17") [41cm (42cm, 43cm)] from bottom. Mark last row for start of armholes. Continue in pattern until piece measures 10½" (11½", 11½") [27cm (29cm, 29cm)] from beginning of armholes. Place first 22 (24, 28) sts on stitch holder for shoulder, place center 28 (30, 30) sts on a separate holder for neck, place remaining 22 (24, 28) sts on a separate holder for second shoulder.

Front
Work the same as for back until piece measures 7½" (8½", 8½") [19cm (21.5, 21.5cm)] from beg of armhole, ending with a WS row.

Begin neck shaping:
Next row: RS: Work first 29 (31, 35) sts in pattern, place center 14 (16, 16) sts on stitch holder for front neck, attach another ball of yarn and work last 29 (31, 35) sts in pattern as established.
Next row: WS: Work each side of neck with separate yarn, working pattern as established.

Decrease at neck edges:
Next row: RS: Work in pattern across all left side sts, drop yarn, on right side, pick up yarn, sl 1 knitwise, work next st in pattern, psso (pass slip stitch over) to bind off 1 st, bind off 2 more sts, work to end of row keeping in pattern as established.
Next row: WS: Work in pattern across all right side sts, drop yarn, on left side, pick up separate yarn, bind off 3 sts as before, work to end of row keeping in pattern as established.
Next row: RS: Maintaining pattern and working each side with separate yarn, bind off 2 sts on neck edge of right side.
Next row: WS: Work across as before, binding off

INCREASING EVENLY ACROSS A ROW

Determine the number of increases needed for your size; for example, 4 for the small sized sleeves (see note below) (see note below). Reserve 4 stitches in which to work the increases. Subtract these sts from the number of sts on the needle (32 for small): 32–4 = 28. Between each increase and the next there will be an even number of sts (called an interval). Between the first and 4th increase (in this example) there are 3 intervals. You have 28 sts left when you exclude the sts where the increases are worked. To find how many sts for each interval, divide 28 by 3 to equal 9 with 1 st left over.

You will have 3 intervals of 9 sts between increases and 1 extra stitch at one end of the row. So you can work the row as follows: Work 1 st, * inc in next st, work 9 sts, repeat from * 2 times more, inc 1 in last. Because this is a ribbing row, you need to work the original stitches in pattern as established, without incorporating the increases into the original ribbing pattern.

(Note: If you choose to increase by working the bar (strand) between existing sts you will not need to reserve a separate st for increases; instead, you will have one more st for each interval and at one end.)

Below
Knitting the last half of the turtleneck on larger needles gives it a soft roll.

2 sts on neck edge of left side.
Repeat these last 2 rows once more.

Sleeves: Make 2
With smaller needles, CO 32 (34, 36) sts, including 2 for selvage (seam allowance).
Work in k1, p1 ribbing for 2" (5cm), increasing 4 sts evenly spaced on last row (*see above*). There are now 36 (38, 40) sts. Change to larger needles.
Establish pattern:
Row 1: RS: K7 (8, 9), for St st, place marker (pm), k1, p1, k1 (seed st), pm, k16, pm, k1, p1, k1, pm, k7 (8, 9).
Row 2: WS: P7 (8, 9), slip marker (sl m), k1, p1, k1, sl m, p16, sl m, k1, p1, k1, sl m, p7 (8, 9).
Repeat these 2 rows once more.
Row 5: RS: K3, inc 1, work in pattern as established to last 4 sts, inc in next st, k3.
Continue to work patterns as established and inc 1 st at each end of row (as for row 5) every 4th row 4 (14, 11) times more, working increased stitches in stockinette st, then inc 1 st each end of row every 6th row 8 (2, 4) times more. Work

Chart for front (or back) of sweater. See cable detail on opposite page.

Right

The detailed pattern that runs the length of the sleeve.

even on 62 (72, 72) sts until sleeve measures 20½" (21", 21½") [about 52cm (53.5cm, 54.5cm)]. Bind off all sts in pattern.

Finishing:

Block pieces. Knit together shoulder seams with three-needle bind-off (*see page 75*). Sew bound-off edge of sleeves to armhole edges between markers. Sew armhole and side seams.

Turtleneck:

With smaller circular needle, transfer k28 (30, 30) sts from back neck. holder onto left-hand needle end and work in pattern as established across them, pick up 14 sts evenly spaced along left front neck edge, transfer and work in pattern across 14 (16, 16) sts from front neck holder, pick up 14 sts evenly spaced along right front neck edge. 70 (74, 74) sts

Round 1: Place marker on needle for beginning of round. * K1, p1, repeat from * to cable on back,

10 Stockinette stitches	3 Seed stitches	8 Stockinette stitches
3 Seed stitches	4 Stockinette stitches	3 Seed stitches

Rows
12
10
8
6
4
2

ending with p1, dec above cable as follows: k2tog, p1, k1, p1, k1, k2tog, p1, then continue in k1, p1 ribbing to front cable, ending with p1, dec above cable as for back, then continue in k1, p1 ribbing to end of round, ending with p1. 66 (70, 70) sts. Work in k1 p1 ribbing as established for 3½" (9cm). Change to larger circular needle. Continue in ribbing until turtleneck measures about 7" (18cm) in length. Bind off all sts in ribbing.

CABLE

| | | | | | | | | | | | | Row 12
Row 12 | | | | — | | | | | | | — | | | | | Row 11
Row 10
| | | | | | | | | | | | | Row 9
Row 8
| | | | — | | | | | | | — | | | |
Row 7 left front cable crossing in front
Row 6 | | | | | | | | | | | | | Row 5
Row 4 | | | | — | | | | | | | — | | | |
| | | | | | | | | | | | | Row 3
Row 2 (WS) | | | | — | | | | | | | — | | | |
| | | | | | | | | | | | | Row 1 (RS)

Garter rib   Garter rib

CODE

| | Knit on RS, Purl on WS (Stockinette Stitch)

| — | Purl on right side, Knit on wrong side (Reverse Stockinette Stitch)

Odd-numbered rows—right side
Read from right to left ◄——————

Even-numbered rows—wrong side
Read from left to right ——————►

SEED STITCH

Row 2 | — | | | — |
| | | — | | | Row 1

10 Cable stitches   3 Seed stitches   4 Stockinette stitches   3 Seed stitches   8 Stockinette stitches   3 Seed stitches   10 Stockinette stitches

Rows

11

9

7

5

3

1

Garter rib   Center of front (or back)   Garter rib

KNITTING FOR YOUNG ONES

Making things for babies and children is a way of sharing in

the joy of the new arrivals and celebrating them as they

grow. Play with texture and color while you are designing!

They'll love whatever you make for them.

———

IT'S A WRAP!

A kimono-style wrap welcomes baby in comfort and style and keeps parents in mind, too. The cardigan, with simple lines and an asymmetrical closure, avoids the need to wrestle the sweater over the infant's head.

Skill level: ◖■□▭
Materials:

Yarn:	Rowan wool cotton, 123yd (112m)/1.75oz (50g) ball
Color:	Citron 901
Amount:	3 (4, 4) balls
Total yardage:	369 (492, 492) yd [336m (448, 448) m]
Needles:	US 6 (4mm) or size to get gauge
Other materials:	Blunt-tipped tapestry needle
Gauge:	24 stitches and 30 rows = 4" (10cm)
Finished size:	3 months, 17½" (44cm) at chest
	6 months, 19" (48cm) at chest
	12 months, 20" (51cm) at chest

The sweater is knitted in one piece, beginning with the back. At the underarm, extra stitches are cast on for the length of each sleeves. After the center stitches are cast off for the back neck, the front of the sweater is knitted in two separate sections, each with its own ball of yarn (*see diagram on page 113*).

INSTRUCTIONS

Back

Cast on 54 (60, 62)sts (number includes 2 sts for selvage).
Garter stitch border:
Rows 1-4: Knit. Border is completed.
Row 5: RS: Knit.

Row 6: WS: Purl.
Continue in stockinette st until piece measures 5" (13cm) ending with WS row.

Cast on for sleeves:
Next row: K to end of row, then cast on 36 (39, 45) sts for sleeve. 90 (93, 99) sts
Next row: K3 for sleeve cuff, p to end, then cast on 36 (39, 45) sts for second sleeve. 126 (138, 152) sts
Next row: RS: Knit.
Establish selvage at sleeve cuff edges:
Next row: WS: With yarn in front (wyif), sl 1 purlwise, pass yarn to back between first 2 sts, k2, p to last 3 sts, k3.
Next row: RS: With yarn in front (wyif), sl 1 purlwise, k to end.
Repeat these two rows until piece measures 8" (9", 10") [20cm (23cm, 25cm)] from bottom, ending with a WS row.
Establish garter st border for back neck:
Next row: Sl 1, k48 (53, 59), place marker (pm) for garter stitch border at back of neck, k28 (30, 32), pm for other side of garter border at back of neck, k remaining 49 (54, 60) sts.
Next row: (WS) Sl 1, k2, p 46 (51, 57), sl m, k 28 (30, 32), sl marker, p 46 (51, 57), k last 3 sts.
Next row: (RS) Sl 1, k all remaining sts.
Next row: Repeat previous WS row.
Shape back of neck:
Next row: (RS) Sl 1, k 48 (53, 59), pm, k 3, bind

off 22 (24, 26) sts for back neck, k 3, pm,
k remaining sts.
Next row: WS: sl 1 wyif, pass yarn to back
between first 2 sts, k2, p to first marker, sl m, k3,
ending at neck edge.
Place right sleeve and right side of sweater on
stitch holder and continue working left sleeve and
left side of sweater only.

Left front and sleeve:
Next row: RS: Sl 1 wyib, k to end.
Next row: WS: Sl 1 wyif, pass yarn to back, k2, p
to marker, k3.
Repeat these two rows twice more, ending on WS
at neck edge.
Begin shaping for left front:
Next row: RS: Sl 1 wyib, k2 (neck border), inc 1
in each of next 2 sts, k to end.
Next row: WS: Sl 1 wyif, sl 1, pass yarn to back,
k2, p to last 3 sts, k3.
Repeat last 2 rows, increasing 2 sts after neck
border as before on RS rows, until sleeve measures

Left
One pair of ties is used to secure
kimono on the inside at the waist.
This holds the garment closed a little
more securely.

7" (18cm) from sleeve cast-on sts, ending with RS
row at sleeve cuff.

Finish shaping left sleeve:
Next row: WS: Maintaining garter stitch border,
bind off 36 (39, 45) sts (first 3 are knit,
remaining sts are purled). Purl until 3 sts remain
on left needle, k 3, turn.
Left front: Continue in St st on left front,
maintaining slipped stitch selvage and garter
stitch border at center edge. At the same time,
continue to increase 2 sts on each right-side row
just after completing garter stitch border at center
edge until there are 45 (49, 51) sts on needle.
Work even (without increasing or decreasing),
until piece measures approx. 4½ (5, 5½)" from
sleeve cast-off, ending with a WS row.
Knit every four rows for garter stitch border. Bind
off.

Right front and sleeve:
Place right sleeve and right front sts on needles
and work to correspond to left front and sleeve,
reversing shaping (*see page 82*).

Finishing:
Block sweater.
Sew sleeve seams with invisible horizontal seam
(*see page 46*), as if they were shoulder seams.
Sew underarm seams using mattress st (invisible
vertical seam, *see page 45*).
Ties:
Short ties: Make 4. Cast on 34 sts. Working each
st as a k st, bind off all sts.
Long ties: Make 2. Cast on 40 sts. Working each
st as a k st, bind off all sts.
Make a small knot at one end of each long tie.
With a tapestry needle threaded with yarn, tack

knotted edge of one long tie to right front about 3½" (9cm) from bottom and 1" (2.5cm) in from center front edge, then secure underside of tie to sweater between knot and front edge. Repeat with other long tie, positioning it about 1½" (4cm) below the first.

Short ties:

Close the sweater with right front overlapping left. With straight pins or yarn thread in tapestry needle, mark position where ties extend beyond the right front edge. Place a short tie on left front opposite each of the right front ties, about 1" (2.5cm) in from front edge as it lies in place. Sew tie ends in place on the left front.

Open the sweater and attach remaining short ties inside, one secured to the seam on the right side of sweater and the other to left front edge, each one about 2½" (6cm) above bottom edge. These inner ties are tied before outer pairs are fastened.

Above
Garter stitch borders add a crisp edge to stockinette stitch, and make it lie flat.

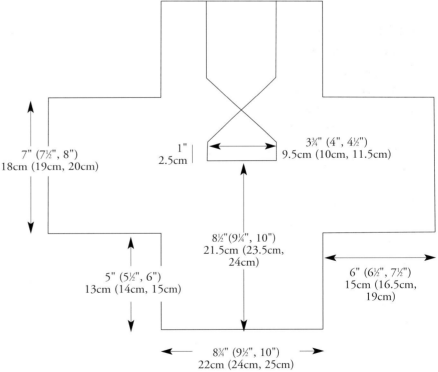

7" (7½", 8")
18cm (19cm, 20cm)

1"
2.5cm

3¾" (4", 4½")
9.5cm (10cm, 11.5cm)

8½" (9¼", 10")
21.5cm (23.5cm, 24cm)

6" (6½", 7½")
15cm (16.5cm, 19cm)

5" (5½", 6")
13cm (14cm, 15cm)

8¾" (9½", 10")
22cm (24cm, 25cm)

BABY BOOTIES

These colorful booties sport high roll-top cuffs and ankle ties that will keep them on baby's feet. Mock "shoelaces" continue across the front.

General Information
Each bootie is worked lengthwise, beginning with a few stitches at the toe that form the platform for a concentration of increases. Once the full width is reached, the bootie is worked up the front and along the sides to the heel. Before any seaming occurs, the decorative shoelaces go on and stitches are picked up around the top of the shoe for the cuff.

Stitch patterns:
Stockinette st: (k 1 row, p 1 row) for upper and cuff; Garter stitch (k every row) for sole.

In the beginning, when your three initial cast-on stitches are called on to multiply themselves four times over in short order, they may balk and try to close up against your needle. Be firm. You are in charge.

INSTRUCTIONS

Shape Toe:
Cast on 3 stitches (sts). Work these early sts loosely enough to accommodate the early increases.
Row 1: Increase 1 in each st. 6 sts
Row 2: Inc 1 in each st. 12 sts
Row 3: RS: K3, inc 1 in next st, place marker (pm) for beginning of upper front, inc 1 in next st, k2, inc 1 in next st, pm for end of upper front, inc 1 in next st, k3. 16 sts

Skill level: ◖◼◼◼◻

Materials:

Yarn:	Debbie Bliss Cashmerino Baby 137yd (125m)/50oz (1.75g) ball
Color:	For Main Color MC, yellow 505 For Contrasting Color (CC), grape 607
Amount:	1 ball each of MC and CC
Total yardage:	274yd (250m)
Needles:	US 6 (4mm) or size to obtain gauge
Other materials	Aluminum crochet hook size E or 4 Tapestry needle
Gauge:	24 stitches and 32 rows = 4" (10cm)
Finished size:	3 to 6 months baby

Row 4: K 4, inc 1 in next st, slip marker (sl m), p6, sl m, inc 1 in next st, k4. 18 sts

Row 5: RS: K6 for sole, sl m, inc 1 in each of next 2 sts, k to last 2 sts before next marker, in 1 in each of next 2 sts, sl m, k6 for sole. 22 sts

Row 6: K6, sl m, p10, sl m, k6.

Row 7: K6, sl m, inc 1 in each of next 3 sts, k4, inc in each of next 3 sts, sl m, k6. 28 sts

Row 8: K6, sl m, p16, sl m, k6.

Row 9: K6, sl m, inc 1 in each of next 2 sts, k12, inc 1 in each of next 2 sts, sl m, k6. 32 sts. Toe shaping is completed.

Row 10: K 6 for sole, sl m, p20 for upper front, sl m, K 6 for sole.

Continue in pattern as established, for 11 more rows, ending with Row 21.

Left
False shoelaces add the final touch to this baby's bootie.

Above
Here you can see the flat seam on the foot of the bootie.

Divide for sides:

Row 22: K6, p8, place next 4 sts on a holder; place remaining 14 sts on a separate holder. Turn and work on 14 sts for one side of bootie.

Row 23: RS: K14

Row 24: K6, p8.

Rows 25–32: Repeat rows 23 and 24 for 4 more times.

Row 33: RS: K14.

Above
The rolled down tops add a
modern look to this baby bootie.

Shape heel:
Row 34: K4, k2tog (decrease made), p8.
Row 35: K8, k2tog; k 3
Row 36: K2, k2tog, p8.
Row 37: K8, k3tog.
Bind off all remaining sts. Cut yarn.
Work the 14 sts of the other side of bootie,
reversing the left-right orientation and heel
shaping, and working garter st on sole sts and
stockinette st on upper front sts, starting with row
22 as follows:
Row 22: WS: P8 for upper front, k6 for sole.
Complete to correspond to first side, reversing
shaping at heel.

Shoelaces:
When second side is completed, work shoelaces
across the front as follows:
Count down 5 rows from the 4 center front sts
still on a stitch holder. The first shoelace will run
across the selected row for the width of those 4
sts. Using the crochet hook and CC yarn, make a
slipknot leaving a tail of several inches. Hold
bootie with RS facing you and hold the slipknot
(with crochet hook removed) and the working
yarn on the WS, under the bootie.

A FLEXIBLE EDGE

I used the cable cast-on for a sturdy, yet flexible
edge. If you tend to cast-on tightly, use a size 7
(4.5mm) needle to put the stitches on and then
go back to a size 6 (4mm) for the knitting. For
the initial concentration of stitch increases,
knitting in the back and front of each stitch
makes the sturdiest toe. If you find it difficult to
get the needle all the way into the stitch a second
time to make an increase, be firm but gentle.

Don't force the right needle into the back of
a stitch too far and risk creating a hole that won't
close up. Instead, work on the tapered parts of
both needle tips. Once the new stitch is made,
gently enlarge it to fit over the full circumference
of the right needle.

After increasing in each stitch for two rows,
you might think your work is horribly stretched
out of shape, but as long as you haven't
manhandled the yarn while making the increases,
the toe will pull together nicely once you've put a
few more rows on the bootie.

Insert hook from RS to WS just to the right of
the first st that the shoelace will cross. Draw the
slip knot through to RS. Then move hook to the
other side of the first st and insert it (RS to WS)
to draw up a loop of working yarn from between
the first two knitted sts to be crossed; draw this
loop through the loop on the crochet hook (chain
st made across first st). Make a chain st in this
manner across each of the 4 designated sts.
To fasten off, draw up a final loop until it is
several inches long. Cut, leaving a long tail.
Thread end in tapestry needle and insert it into
work just outside the last chain st to secure its
loop as you fasten off the yarn end on the WS.
Make an identical shoelace 4 rows below the first.

Cuff:

With RS of work facing you, using CC, begin at heel to pick up 14 sts on one side of bootie, pick up and k center 4 sts (from holder), pick up 14 sts along other side of bootie to heel. 32sts
Next row: WS: With CC, purl.
Next row (eyelet row): RS: Attach MC. * K2, yo, k2tog (eyelet made), repeat from * 7 times more.
Next row: P across 32 sts, including yarn-overs. Continuing in stockinette st, work 2 rows CC, 2 rows MC, 2 rows CC, 2 rows MC, 8 rows CC. Bind off all sts.

Finishing:

For each bootie, sew a flat seam up bottom of sole and back of heel, picking up edge stitches from side to side. The flat seam eliminates the selvage which might irritate baby's foot. Here's how to do do this type of seam. With right sides out, insert a tapestry needle back to front in the garter stitch bumps at the outer edges on alternating sides. At the heel, turn the bootie inside out. Continue working edge to edge on the reverse side of stockinette stitch.

Ties: Make 2.
With crochet hook and CC, crochet a chain (*see page 86*) about 13" (33cm) long. Starting and ending at center front, weave the ties through the eyelets on the cuff. Tie the ends in a bow.

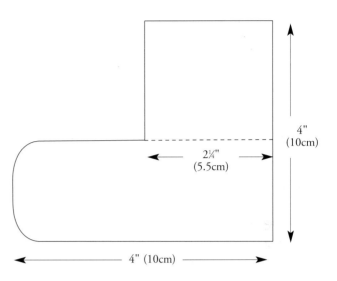

Right
High roll-tops, false shoelaces, and ties threaded through eyelets are both practical are great design features.

MOSAIC KNITTING

Mosaic knitting, named for the geometric effect of some of the patterns, is a clever way of achieving the look of a two-color pattern without having to manage two strands of yarn or switch from one color to another in the middle of a row.

Long after I had learned to do many fancy things with knittting stitches, I could not shake my fear of changing colors in the middle of a row. I wish I had known then about the fun I could have using a simple short-cut called Mosaic Knitting, or Two-color, Slip-stitch Knitting.

This kind of knitting differs from the two major types of colorwork, Intarsia and Fair Isle. In Fair Isle, one color shows in small clusters of just a few stitches—usually from one to five— while one or more additional colors travel across each row on the wrong side, waiting for their turn to move up to the front.

Intarsia lends itself to a more painterly effect. Each color stays within the space assigned by a chart that allows one square for each stitch. In the color change, the old and new strands are twisted around each other on the wrong side to prevent holes from forming in the fabric.

Mosaic knitting, invented about 35 years ago by Barbara G. Walker, offers an easier way of mixing splashes of color. This technique merges two-row stripes with patterns that feature slipped stitches. Creating a stripe effect is as easy as attaching a new ball of yarn. And slipping a stitch simply means moving it from the left needle to the right needle without working it. Put the two together and you get a series of slip stitches punctuating the stripes.

To set up a pattern, start with a one-row stripe on the wrong side of the work. This is a preparation row, a row that is not technically part of the stitch pattern but does some essential foundation work. Assuming that you are working in stockinette stitch —the most common stitch in mosaic knitting—the preparation row will be a purl row. For this discussion, we'll use the pink and purple colors as in the child's cardigan on the following pages.

In the first bit of mosaic, which appears on the sleeves of the child's cardigan, the preparation row is purled in pink. When you turn the work to the right side for the first row in the pattern, the pink preparation row will provide the source for slipped stitches. The purple yarn will do the actual knitting.

The first and last stitches in each row are worked regardless of the pattern. They anchor the yarn, and any pattern irregularities they might produce are hidden inside the seams.

Mosaic patterns are charted. The charts in the next project use one square for each stitch. Slipped stitches are blank, or white, space which indicates an absence of knitting. Stitches that are worked up appear as a color or symbol.

If you are working the first of the two mosaic patterns in the next project, you will knit the first stitch in purple and slip the second one, which is pink, from the row below. Slip it purlwise so the stitch doesn't get twisted. The working yarn travels across the wrong side of the slipped stitches until it is needed. With the right side facing, the working yarn travels in back. When the wrong side of the piece faces you, the working yarn floats in front.

Once you've completed the first row of the mosaic pattern, you need only to look at the stitches on your needles to guide you back across the return row. If the stitch on the row below is purple, purl. If it's pink, slip it purlwise a second time. A slipped stitch elongates to keep up with its companions. It can take this sort of treatment for a maximum of two rows without distorting the fabric. In the third and fourth rows, pink and purple must reverse roles, with pink becoming the working yarn and the purple yarn providing the slipped stitches.

Mosaic knitting has its advantages and limitations, just like anything else. The best results come from using fibers that bounce back and keep their shape, although that doesn't mean the project must be made of wool. For example, the sweater is knitted with cotton. Mosaic patterns, involving a relatively small number of stitches, do not lend themselves to interpreting large blocks of color. But for the novice, mosaic knitting builds confidence. It gives you a chance to try the idea of Fair Isle with just one strand of yarn floating across a row. When you have completed it, you'll see that blocking minimizes any uneven stitches that may have crept into the work along the way.

Left
Mixing rows of colored yarn becomes a major design feature in a garment, as this photograph of the child's cardigan (on following pages) shows.

A GIRL'S CARDIGAN

This girl's cardigan in rich jewel tones captures the look

of fair isle without the intricate work.

Knit some, slip some. That's the key for achieving two-color knitting without having to carry two strands across the back of the work. Slip-stitch patterns in two colors, also called mosaic knitting, are usually worked in stockinette stitch.

Before you begin, take time to make a swatch and check your guage. Then you will be sure to get the required size.

INSTRUCTIONS

Back

With color A, cast on 56 (62, 68) stitches, including two selvage stitches.
Work in k1, p1 ribbing for six rows.
Next row: Knit.
Next row: Purl.
Continue in stockinette stitch for 4 more rows (12 rows in all completed). Drop A.
Next row: RS: Attach B and knit across row. Drop B.
Next row: WS: Attach C and purl across row.
Next row: RS: Lay A over C at the side, bring C up from under A and with C knit across row.
Next row: WS: Lay B over C, bring C up from under B and with C purl across row.
With C, work 2 more rows in stockinette stitch, bringing unused colors up the sides in the manner described. Cut C, leaving several inches to weave in tail.
Next row: RS: With A, knit across row. Cut A,

TWO GOOD TIPS

One rule in mosaic knitting is that the first and last stitch of each row is knit or purled to anchor the color in use, regardless of the pattern.

Make sure the slipped stitches are spread out on the right needle before picking up the working yarn to knit or purl the next stitch. If the slipped stitches are too close together, the fabric will draw inward and pucker, and blocking will not help.

Skill level:	■■■□
Materials:	
Yarn:	Mission Falls 1824 Cotton, 84yd (77m)/1.75oz (50g) ball
Colors:	For A, Aubergine 407
	For B, Lilac 406
	For C, Cosmos 203
Amount:	For A, 4 (5, 6) balls
	For B, 2 balls
	For C, 1 ball
Total yardage:	About 336yd (420, 504)yd [306m (385, 462)m] for A, 168yd (153m) for B, 84yd (77m) for C, or about 588yd (536m) in all sizes
Needles:	US 9 (5.5mm) or size to obtain gauge
Other materials:	6 buttons
Gauge:	17 stitches and 22 rows = 4" (10cm)
Finished size:	Size 2 (4, 6) years; 26" (29", 32") at chest

leaving a tail to be woven in.
Next row: WS: Pick up B from under A tail and with B, purl across row.
Next row: RS: With B, knit.
Continue working with B in stockinette stitch for 7 rows more, ending with WS row. Cut B, leaving tail.
Attach A. Work in stockinette stitch until piece measures 8½" (9", 9½") [21.5cm (23cm, 24cm)] Mark last row for underarms. Continue working even (without inc or dec) in St st until piece measures 13¼" (14", 15") [33.5cm (35.5cm, 38cm)] ending with WS row.

Neck shaping

First row: RS: Knit 18 (19, 22) stitches, place marker (pm), join new ball of yarn, and knit 20 (24, 24) stitches. Place these center 20 (24, 24) sts on stitch holder, k remaining 18 (19, 22) sts. Work each side of neck with its separate ball of yarn as follows:
Next row: WS: Purl across one side of neck, drop

yarn; on other side of neck, pick up other ball of yarn and sl 1 st purlwise, p1, pass slipped st over, (psso—1 dec made), purl to end. 17 (18, 21) sts on last side.

Next row: RS: K17; on other side, sl 1, k1, psso (skp—one dec made), k to end. 17 (18, 21) sts remain on each side.

For smallest and middle sizes, repeat last 2 rows once more. 16 (17) sts remain on each side of neck. For largest size, work even for two rows. Next row for all sizes, p. Bind off shoulder stitches on each side, or put stitches on holders for three-needle bind-off.

Left front:

Note: Directions are for a girl's cardigan. For a boy's cardigan, with colors of your choosing, knit the Right Front first, omitting buttonholes. then work Left Front, adding buttonholes, worked on the 3rd and 4th sts in from the center front edge. With A, cast on 30 (33, 36) sts.

Row 1: RS: * P1, k1, repeat from * to end. Repeat this row 5 more times.

Now work in stockinette stitch with built-in button band as follows:

Row 1: RS: K to last 4 (4, 4) sts, place marker (pm), p1, k1, p1, k1.

Row 2: WS: P1, k1, p1, k1, slip marker (sl m), p to end.

Continue in stockinette st and ribbed button

Left

The top of the sleeve is knitted in a unique design, and then it is inserted into the armhole.

band at center front edge for 4 more rows with color A, then work:

1 row B,

5 rows C,

1 row A,

9 rows B.

Carry unused colors up the sides of the work if they will be used again. When they are no longer needed, cut yarn, leaving a tail. When stripes are completed, work with A only.

Continue to work stockinette st and ribbed button band until piece measures 8½" (9, 9½") [21.5cm (23cm, 24cm)]. Mark last row for underarm. Continue working even for 3¾" (4" , 4½") [9.5cm (10cm, 11.5cm)] more ending with RS row at center front. Piece measures 12¼" (13", 14") [31cm (33cm, 35.5cm)] from beginning.

Neck shaping:

Next row: WS: Work first 9 (11, 11) sts at neck edge and place them onto stitch holder, p to end.

Next row: RS: Knit.

Next row: WS: Sl 1, p1, psso, bind off 2 more sts, p to end.

Next row: (RS): K.

Next row: For smallest and middle sizes only: (WS): Sl 1, p1, psso, bind off 1 more st, p to end

Next row: For largest size only: (WS): Sl 1, p1, psso, p to end.

Work even on 16 (17, 21) sts until length of front matches back to shoulders. Bind off or put stitches in holder for three-needle bind-off later.

Right front

With A, cast on 30 (33, 36) sts.

Row 1: RS: * K1, p1, repeat from * to end.

Repeat this row 3 times more.

Make first of six buttonholes as follows:

Row 5: K1, p1, k2tog, yo (buttonhole made), *
k1, p1, repeat from * to end.

Row 6: Work in ribbing as established, making a
k st in the yarn-over of the previous row. Plan
spacing for remaining 5 buttonholes, marking the
buttonband on the completed front as a guide.
The first buttonhole (just completed) is about 1"
(2.5cm) above bottom edge, the last buttonhole
will be about 1/2" (1.25cm) from top of the
neckband ribbing with the remaining 4 evenly
spaced between (see Buttonholes, page 55).
Making buttonholes on ribbed band to
correspond to the left front markings (counting
rows carefully), work right front to correspond to
left front, reversing shaping (see Reverse Shaping,
page 82).

Sleeves:

Make 2.

With A, cast on 30 (32, 32) st

Work 6 rows ribbing as for back.

Row 7: RS: Knit and inc 1 st at each end of row.

Rows 8-10: Starting with a p row, work even in St
st on 32 (34, 34) sts.

Row 11: RS: Repeat Row 7. 34 (36, 36) sts

Row 12: Purl.

Begin stripes, carrying unused colors up (that are
dropped and not cut) side edges of work as
before.

Row 13: Drop A, attach B and k across. Drop B.

Row 14: Attach C and p across.

Row 15: With C, k across, inc 1 st each end. 36
(38, 38) sts

Rows 16-18: With C, work even in St st.

Row 19: Drop C, pick up A and k across, inc 1 st
each end. Cut A, leaving tail. 38 (40, 40) sts

Row 20: With B, p across.

Rows 21-22: With B, work even in St st.

Row 23: With B, k across, increasing 1 st each
end for large size only. 38 (40, 42) sts

Rows 24: With B, p.

Row 25-26: With B, work in St st.

Row 27: With B, k across, increasing 1 st each end
40 (42, 44) sts

Row 28: With B, p across. Drop B.

Row 29: Attach A, and k across. Cut A, leaving tail.

Row 30: Preparation row for mosaic colorwork:
Attach C and p across.

Cut C, leaving tail.

Row 31: With B, k1 and inc in this first st, sl 1 st
with yarn in back (wyib), * k1, sl 1wyib, repeat
from * until last 2 sts, k and inc in next st, k1. 42
(44, 46) sts

Row 32, With B, k1, then with yarn in front
(wyif), p the B sts (that were knitted on previous
row) and sl the C sts (that were slipped on
previous row), ending k last st.

Rows 33-34: With B, work even in St st on all sts.
Drop B.

Row 35: Attach A and k across, increasing 1 st
each end. 44 (46, 48) sts

Row 36: Preparation row for mosaic colorwork:
Attach C and p across. Drop C.

Row 37: With B, k1, sl 1 wyib, * k1, sl 1 wyib,
repeat from * until last st, k1.

Row 38: With B, k1, repeat row 32.

Rows 39-52. With B, work in St st and AT THE
SAME TIME, inc 1st in first and last sts on Rows
39, 43, and 47. 50 (52, 54) sts

Row 53: With C, k1 (2, 1), sl 0 (0, 1) wyib, * k1, sl
5 wyib, repeat from * to last 8 (3, 4) sts, k1, sl 5 (1,
2) wyib, k2 (1, 1).

Row 54: With C, k1, then wyif, sl B sts (slipped on
previous row) and p C sts (knitted on previous row),
ending with k last st. Drop C.

Row 55: With B, k6 (1, 2), * sl 1 wyib, k5, repeat
from * to last 2 (3, 4) sts, sl 1 wyib, k1 (2, 3).

Row 56: With B, k1, then p all B sts knitted on
previous row and, wyif, sl all C sts slipped on
previous row to last st, k last st. Drop B.

Row 57: With C, k2 (3, 4), * sl 3 wyib, k3, repeat
from * to last 6 (7, 2) sts, sl 3 (3, 1) wyib, k3 (4, 1).

Row 58: With C, k1, then p all C sts knitted on last
row and, wyif, sl all B sts slipped on previous row to
last st, k last st. Drop C.

Row 59: With B, k1, sl 1 (2, 3) wyib, * k3, sl 3

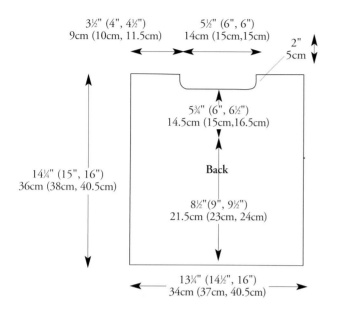

3½" (4", 4½")
9cm (10cm, 11.5cm)

5½" (6", 6")
14cm (15cm,15cm)

2"
5cm

5¾" (6", 6½")
14.5cm (15cm,16.5cm)

Back

14¼" (15", 16")
36cm (38cm, 40.5cm)

8½"(9", 9½")
21.5cm (23cm, 24cm)

13¼" (14½", 16")
34cm (37cm, 40.5cm)

CHART ONE

First gap mosaic sequence on sleeves
1 pattern repeat is 2 stitches wide
White space means stitches immediately below (pink)
are slipped without being worked.

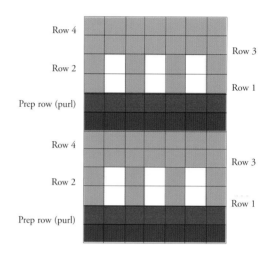

Row 4

Row 2

Row 3

Row 1

Prep row (purl)

Row 4

Row 2

Row 3

Row 1

Prep row (purl)

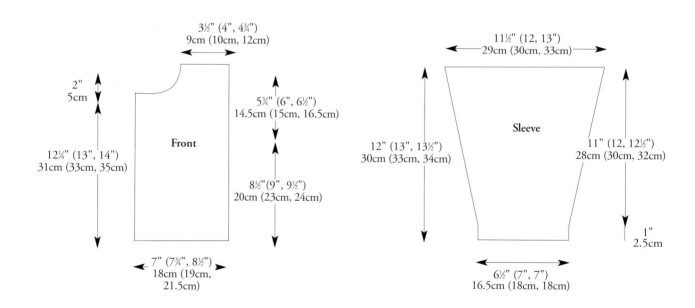

3½" (4", 4¾")
9cm (10cm, 12cm)

2"
5cm

5¾" (6", 6½")
14.5cm (15cm, 16.5cm)

Front

12¼" (13", 14")
31cm (33cm, 35cm)

8½"(9", 9½")
20cm (23cm, 24cm)

7" (7¾", 8½")
18cm (19cm, 21.5cm)

11½" (12, 13")
29cm (30cm, 33cm)

Sleeve

12" (13", 13½")
30cm (33cm, 34cm)

11" (12, 12½")
28cm (30cm, 32cm)

1"
2.5cm

6½" (7", 7")
16.5cm (18cm, 18cm)

CHART TWO

Top of sleeves
Shows 2 full pattern repeats (in width)

Purple = light purple
White space = stitches in colour immediately below are slipped without working

V	V	V		V	V	V	V	V		V	V	V	
V	V	V		V	V	V	V	V		V	V	V	Row 9, 10 work pink, slip purple
	∧	∧	∧			∧	∧	∧					
	∧	∧	∧			∧	∧	∧					Row 7, 8 work purple, slip pink
V	V			V	V	V				V	V		
V	V			V	V	V				V	V		Row 5, 6 work pink, slip purple
	∧	∧	∧	∧	∧		∧	∧	∧	∧	∧		
	∧	∧	∧	∧	∧		∧	∧	∧	∧	∧		Row 3, 4 work light purple, slip pink
V					V						V		Row 2
V					V						V		Row 1, 2 work pink, slip purple
∧	∧	∧	∧	∧	∧	∧	∧	∧	∧	∧	∧	∧	Prep Row

Last/first stitch always worked   Last/first stitch always worked

wyib, repeat from * to last 6 (7, 5) sts, k3, sl 2 (3, 1), k1.

Row 60: With B, k1, then wyif, sl all C sts slipped on previous row and p all B sts knitted on previous row to last st, k last st. Cut B, leaving a tail.

Row 61: With C, k3 (4, 5), * sl 1 wyib, k5, repeat from * to last 5 (6, 7) sts, sl 1 wyib, k4 (5, 6).

Row 62: With C, k1, then p all C sts knitted on previous row and, wyif, sl all B sts slipped on previous row to last st, k last st.
Cut C, leaving a tail.

Attach A and work in St st until piece measures 12" (13", 13½") [30cm (33cm, 34cm)]. There will be ½" (1½", 2") [1.25cm (3.75cm, 5cm)] of A above the top design.]

Bind off all sts.

Finishing

Sew or k together shoulder seams in three-needle bind off. Sew sleeve seams. (Sleeve increases were put in edge sts to avoid problems in color pattern, so mattress st seam won't be invisible.) Sew side seams.

Neckband:

With RS facing you and using A, pick up 9 (11, 11) sts on right front, 11 sts along curve on right front, 20 (24, 24) sts from holder at back of neck, 11 sts along curve on left front, and 9 (11, 11) sts on left front. 60 (68, 68) sts

Next row: With inside of sweater facing you, * p1, k1, repeat from * to end, ending with p1.

Next row: Make buttonhole: k1, p1, k2tog, yo, *k1, p1, repeat from * to end.

Work 2 more rows in ribbing as established. Bind off in ribbing. Sew on buttons opposite buttonholes. (For a boy's sweater, work buttonhole on the left side, at end of RS row.)

INDEX

A
abbreviations 58
acrylic fibres 15
alpaca yarn 14
angora 14

B
babies clothes 108–17
baby yarn 15
backstitches 46
bags
   evening 84–7
   knitting 21
balls of yarn, working
   with 16
bar increase 33
binding off 32
   three-needle 75
blocking 44, 70, 113
boatneck sweater
   68–71
bobbins 19, 118
body measurements 40
booties, baby 114–17
borders 54–5
bulky yarn 15
buttonholes 55

C
cable cast-on 26
cardigans
   casual 80–3
   girl's 120–5
care instructions
   on yarn band 17
   garments 59
cashmere 14

casting-on 24–6
chain stitch 86
chenilles 15
children's clothes
   108–25
chunky yarn 15
circular needles 18,
   20–1
coils of yarn, working
   with 16
color
   intarsia 118–19
   yarn label
     information 17
cotton yarn 14
crochet hook 18

D
decreases 34–5
double knitting (DK)
   yarn 15
double stitch 31
double-pointed needles
   18, 21, 97
   casting on 25
dropped stitches 51–2
drying garments 59
dye lots 17

E
earflaps, hat with 94–7
embellishments 54–5
equipment 18–19
errors, correcting 50–3
evening bag 84–7
eyelet buttonholes 55

F
fastening off 32
fibre content, yarn band
   information 17
fingering yarn 15
fit 39–41
flexible edges 116
fringed scarf 62–3
fringes 62, 78

G
garter stitches 30
gauge 70
   label information 17
   markers 19
glossary 56–7
grafting 83
graph paper 19

H
hanks of yarn, working
   with 16
hats
   circular 94–7
   rolled brim 66–7
holding yarn 29

I
I-cords 55
increases 33–4
invisible seams 45, 46

J
joining 92

K
knit stitches 27
   dropped 51
   twisted 50
   unraveling 51
knitting bags 21

L
labels, yarns 17
left-slanting decreases
   35
lifted increase 34
lightweight yarns 15
linen yarn 14
long-tail cast on 24

M
make one 33
markers
   gauge 19
   stitch 19
mattress stitch 45–7
measuring 74
microfibers 15
mohair 14
moss stitch 31

N
natural yarns 14
needles
   choosing 19
   circular 18, 20–1
   double-pointed 18,
     21, 97
   point protectors 18
   size chart 19
   size information 17

straight 18
tapestry 18
types 18, 20–1
notebooks 19
novelty yarns 15
nylon 15

O
openwork scarf 88–9
overcasting 47

P
patterns
  abbreviations 58
  reading 38
  terms in 56–7
picking up 48–9, 53
pins 19
plies 15
point protectors 18
polyamide 15
polyester fiber 15
ponchos 76–9
purl stitches 28
  decreases 35
  dropped 52
  twisted 50
  unraveling 51

R
rayon 15
reverse shaping 82
reverse stockinette
  stitches 30
ribbing 31
ribbon yarn 15, 65
rolled brim hat 66–7

S
scarves
  fringed 62–3
  openwork 88–9
  silken 64–5
scissors 19
seaming 45
seed stitches 31
selvage 70, 75
shaping 33
  reverse 82
silk yarn 14
single crochet 54
sizing 39–41
skeins of yarn, working
  with 16
slip knots 24
slip stitch 54
sport weight yarn 15
stitch gauges 36–7
stitch holders 18
stitch markers 19
stitches
  backstitches 46
  casting on 24–6
  chain 86
  double seed stitch 31
  evening up 31
  garter 30
  knit stitch 27
  mattress 45
  moss 31
  picking up 48–9
  purl 28
  reverse stockinette 30
  seed 31

single crochet 54
slip 54
stockinette 30
stockinette stitches 30
storing garments 59
straight needles 18
style 39
substitutions, yarns 16
summer top, sleeveless
  72–5
swatches 36, 39
sweater, boatneck 68–9
synthetic yarns 15

T
tape measures 18
tapestry needles 18
three-needles bind-off
  75
thumb cast-on 25
tools 18–19
turtleneck topper 90–3
twisted knit stitches 50
twisted purl stitches 50
two-ply yarns 15
two-strand tip 87

U
unravelling 51–2

W
washing garments 59
weights, yarns 15, 17
winding yarn 16
wool 14
worsted weight 15
wrap, baby's 110–13

Y
yarn over 34
yarns 14–17
  holding 29
  labels 17
  natural 14
  selection 16
  substitutions 16
  synthetic 15
  types 14–15
  weights 15, 17
  winding 16
  working with 16

ACKNOWLEDGMENTS

This book would not have been possible without the vision and guidance of Lynn Bryan, who has led me on a path of discovery and excitement while keeping everything in focus. Thanks also to Margery Winter and Deana Gavioli of Berroco, Inc. and to Joelle Meier Rioux at Rowan Yarns for their generosity and support; the photographer, the book designer and to editor Ellen Liberles for keeping me on track.

Wonderfully generous knitters have lent their expertise and invaluable comments to this project; Nancy Henderson, Kim Conteiro of Bella Yarns; Fran Scullin, Lindsay Woodel, Peg Nardacci, Deb Gerhardt, Angela Medici, Ellen Longo, Ann McGarry, Elaine Boyd, Carrie Weinstein, and Roni Phipps.

The staff at Sakonnet Purls—Louise Silverman, Alex Silverman, Stephanie Walmsley, Lorraine Tribble and Nancy Emes—made me feel like I have a second home. Thanks! I'm also grateful to Debbie Schmeller and Anne Luginbuhl for their knitting stories.

Last, but never least, thanks to the three guys closest to my heart: my husband, Larry, and my sons, Mike, just for understanding, and Jeff, for lending his artistic gifts.

RESOURCES

Berroco Inc.
P.O. Box 367
Uxbridge, MA 01569
USA
In Canada Berroco is distributed
by S.R. Kertzer, Ltd.

Debbie Bliss
Gedifra
Distributed by
Knitting Fever Inc.
P.O. Box 502
Roosevelt, NY 11575-0502

Lana Grossa
Distributed by Unicorn Books
   and Crafts
1338 Ross Street
Petaluma, CA 94954

Mission Falls
Distributed by
Unique Kolours
28 North Bacton Hill Rd.
Malvern, PA 19355

Reynolds
Distributed by JCA
35 Scales Lane
Townsend, MA 01469

Rowan Yarns
4 Townsend West, Unit 8
Nashua, NH 03063

Tahki Yarns
Distributed by
Tahki· Stacy Charles, Inc
8000 Cooper Ave.
Glendale, NY 11385

In Canada and the United
Kingdom:

Debbie Bliss
Distributed by Designer Yarns
Newbridge Interbrough Estate
Unit 8-10, Pitt Street
Keighley, West Yorkshire
BD21 4PQ

Rowan Yarns
Green Lane Mill
Holmfirth
West Yorks HD7 1RW.

S.R. Kertzer, Ltd.
105A Winges Road
Woodbridge ON L4L 6C2.

Accessories:
Buttons for evening bag, p85 and
child's cardigan, p121
Sakonnet Purls
3988 Main Rd.
Tiverton, RI 02878.

Button for woman's cardigan,
   page 80
Bella Yarns
508 Main St.
Warren, RI 02885.